YOUTH VOICE PROJECT

STUDENT INSIGHTS INTO BULLYING AND PEER MISTREATMENT

STAN DAVIS AND CHARISSE L. NIXON

RESEARCH PRESS
PUBLISHERS

2612 North Mattis Avenue, Champaign, Illinois 61822
800.519.2707 / researchpress.com

RESEARCH PRESS
PUBLISHERS

Copyright © 2014 by Stan Davis and Charisse Nixon

5 4 3 2 1   13 14 15 16 17

Copies of this book may be ordered from Research Press at the address given on the title page.

Composition by Jeff Helgesen
Cover design by McKenzie Wagner, Inc.
Printed by Bradford & Bigalow

ISBN 978-0-87822-681-8
Library of Congress Control Number 2013951942

Contents

Figures and Tables

Figures

Tables

Preface

We—Stan Davis and Charisse Nixon—met many years ago at an International Bullying Prevention Association conference where we were both making separate training presentations. We have since presented in parallel at many conferences, including several put on by the Ophelia Project. We recognized two common threads in each other's work. First, each of us is continually searching to learn and disseminate better methods for improving children's lives. Second, each of us combines a deep respect for scientific research with a quest for practical solutions, solutions that can be implemented in real schools and communities.

We began the Youth Voice Project because we wanted to know what really helps young people who have been bullied and mistreated by peers. Advice is often given to bullied youth, to peers who observe bullying, and to adults who see or hear about bullying. Young people are sometimes told that they should ignore bullying or confront those who do cruel things to them. Youth who are aware of bullying are often told that they should confront those who do it. Adults get a bewildering range of advice, from staying uninvolved so youth learn how to solve their own problems to using consequences to stop the behavior. We first searched for other studies that had asked large numbers of young people what helped when they were bullied or mistreated. The literature was sparse. As a result, we decided to begin this study. Our primary goal was to bring the voices and experiences of youth themselves into the national dialogue about bullying. This book, then, is our effort to represent the perspectives of youth—and to bridge the gap between research findings and applied work. Too often, research studies are confined to academic journals and libraries; seldom are they applied to optimize students' development. The majority of applied work also remains isolated and is often perceived by academics as "sloppy science," loosely based on the scientific method. If written for the educator or caring adult, the focus tends to be more on individual case studies and general knowledge, with very limited supporting statistics. On the other hand, if written for the academic, the focus tends to rest primarily on the statistics, with limited general commentary and relevant case studies. Knowing there is value in both qualitative and quantitative work, we decided early on that one of the major goals of this book would be to integrate the approaches. In other words, we hope to provide the reader with both genuine student voices as well as empirical data collected from a survey of a large population of children and youth from all over the United States.

We have found our collaboration productive and enjoyable, and hope that the information and techniques we will present in this book will equip you to help youth live better lives. Because the issue of bullying and peer mistreatment is ultimately personal, we would like to share some personal history by way of explaining our deep interest in this difficult subject. We invite you to examine your own history as well—everyone has a story to share.

STAN'S STORY

My own early experiences of young people mistreating their peers began in kindergarten and continued through high school. I taught myself to read before I began attending school by listening to my grandmother as she read me the same books over and over and by watching her finger point to the words. Gradually, I broke the code and connected the black squiggles on the page with the words she was reading. When the teachers at my school learned that I could already read, they brought me to the upper grade classes and put me on display. I remember vividly my pride as they told the sixth graders: "This boy reads better than some of you—and he's only in kindergarten." In the pride I felt at that moment, I did not foresee the sixth graders' reaction to this message, which I see now was intended to shame the older students into working harder. The second half of this memory involves going out to recess afterward and being hit and knocked down by those same sixth graders. I remember refusing to read in class and refusing to do schoolwork, to the point where I was given intelligence testing to see why I was not learning. As my elementary school years continued, I continued to be hit and ostracized by most of my peers. Though I had dialed back my academic achievements, peers began focusing on my overweight body shape and my poor eye-hand coordination. I realize now that I probably had some kind of visual-motor learning disability: My handwriting was illegible no matter how hard I tried to improve it, and I was unable to throw or hit a ball with anything approaching accuracy. This last difficulty was a serious bar to social acceptance in my peer world of the 1950s. Striking out in softball or baseball or missing a catch in the field was enough to brand a young person a loser. The derogatory nickname "Stan the Man Unusual" stuck, and I remember endless games of keep away on the playground as I saw valued belongings of mine thrown from peer to peer. When I ran after these belongings, other kids would trip me and laugh.

Why is it important to think about or tell these stories? The details of our own experiences, and those of others, help us see what peer mistreatment is. People's experiences help us understand how harm can be done. People's experiences help us see what not to do about this problem. And, most important, people's experiences of what worked for them help us see what to do. In my work with peer mistreatment as a therapist and in schools for more than four decades, I have been informed by my own experiences and by the struggles and triumphs of youth and educators. In that work, I have done my best to be guided by Donald Schon's 1983 book *The Reflective Practitioner: How Professionals Think in Action*. Schon presents clearly the crucial idea that we can claim to be professionals only if we continually evaluate the actions and interventions we use. He stresses the need for clear outcome goals and conscious reflection about whether the interventions we are using are actually reaching those goals. The other choice, Schon explains, is for us to continue to use the techniques that we have been taught with no regard for whether they are reaching our goals.

What are our goals in bullying prevention? We will address that question in more detail as we present what thousands of youth told us about their experiences. For now, let me suggest some goals: First, young people who are mistreated need adults to stop the mistreatment if it is within their power. There must have been adults on duty on my elementary school playground, though I do not remember them. When I was lying on the ground crying through a bloody nose, that could have been seen as a sign that other students shouldn't be allowed to hit or trip me, yet I do not remember any effort to stop the other students' behavior. To bring this same issue to the world of today, I have heard from many youth and teachers about anti-gay slurs being used frequently in the hearing of adults without the adults' saying or doing anything. One particularly courageous high school freshman in a town near me in Maine wrote a pledge and took it to each teacher at his school, asking each teacher to commit to saying something to stop the "That's so gay" negative comments he—and they—were hearing all day. He returned to some of the teachers over and over, pointing out the number of their professional peers who had signed the pledge and finally, through persistence, got a majority of the teachers to make this commitment.

Young people who are mistreated by their peers are very likely to be socially isolated. Reducing isolation involves conscious efforts to build peer and adult connections for all. As I see it, this is not because most mistreated youth begin their childhoods with social skill deficiencies. Instead, youth who are members of groups who are not valued by the school community are more likely to be mistreated and ostracized socially. You will see both these effects—increased mistreatment and decreased school connectedness—in our research results. There is one more reason that mistreated youth tend to be socially isolated. Students who are mistreated and ostracized from early childhood miss the opportunity to develop age-appropriate social skills, which are learned in positive interactions. Thus, by adolescence, they may appear socially awkward because they have not had the opportunity to learn how to socialize comfortably with others. Addressing this isolation requires different interventions in addition to stopping mean behavior. As I examine my own memories of peer interaction during my teen years, I remember little overt name-calling or physical aggression. Yet I remember consistent social ostracism, which had a deep effect. If we focus only on stopping overt mistreatment and not on building social inclusion, we may not help excluded youth.

It is important for adults to work for equity and fairness for subgroups within schools. As I have described in the last paragraphs, some groups are devalued in many schools. These young people include but are not limited to overweight youth; gifted students; youth with learning difficulties; youth who do not fit stereotyped gender roles; gay, lesbian, bisexual, and transgendered (GLBT) students; youth in racial, ethnic, or religious minorities; and others. This devaluing of subgroups legitimizes mistreatment of young people in those groups and strengthens societally learned bias and prejudice. It is important that schools examine and work to reduce devaluing of youth and groups. We will be addressing methods for promoting equity in more depth in this book.

Because we will never be completely successful in changing peers' interactions and in promoting inclusion and equity, it is important for adults to do everything we can to build resiliency in youth. Young people will experience peer rejection, mistreatment, and failure. Although we should do everything in our power to prevent negative events, we must also help youth not to blame themselves for the mean actions of others. As a student told me years ago, "First they bully you, then you bully yourself." He was describing his own internal thought processes, in which he internalized others' criticism and berated himself for being inadequate. We can help young people break this chain of events and choose not to be harmed by others' negative opinions of them. From my experience, both personal and professional, covering the 60 years from kindergarten to now, I believe that building resiliency in youth—like protecting youth from negative behavior—is important but not sufficient in itself. Efforts to reduce mean behavior *and* efforts to build inner strength are necessary if we want young people to grow up strong and self-confident.

Let's return to my story. In the 1950s, I don't remember hearing the word *bullying.* My experience of mistreatment and ostracism, and the reactions of the few adults I told about what had happened to me, taught me two things: This was my fault, and it wasn't going to change. When I told adults, they asked me why I had not hit back. When I asked to stay in at recess, teachers told me I needed to get exercise. As children will, I accepted this reality: I was going to be called names and shunned. I was going to be chosen last for activities after a theatrical effort to find someone else who could be chosen instead of me. I was going to be hit.

I withdrew into books, the guitar, and fantasies. I read Alexandre Dumas' epic revenge novel *The Count of Monte Cristo* over and over again, relishing the fantasy of the mistreated Edmond Dantés returning to his tormentors as a wealthy, respected instrument of vengeance. I read Arthur Conan Doyle's Sherlock Holmes books, admiring this highly intelligent and socially awkward detective whom people had to respect because of his abilities. In my late teens and early twenties, I found my first real connections with peers through social justice activities, through music, and through a love of the outdoors. I found an adult mentor in the father of an ex-girlfriend, who encouraged me and kept me from despair over 30 years of occasional dinners and letters. I fell in love and raised a family, and settled in a small town where I have a large web of positive connections. I continue to play music and connect with a community of musicians, and I continue to read books that remind me that social outcasts can have good lives. To Dumas and Conan Doyle, I would add Katherine Paterson's novels, J. K. Rowling's Harry Potter books, and many others.

What worked for me during my socially isolated childhood and adolescence? What stopped me in adolescence from becoming addicted to alcohol or other drugs or from killing myself? These are relevant questions. As I look back, I see that I was at significant risk for both outcomes. I drank heavily, starting at age

15 or so, and included other drugs in that pattern as those became available to me in the mid- 1960s. I went through several phases of serious suicidal thinking, including specific plans for death, in my late teens at college. As I look back, at the root of both these risk patterns were two beliefs: I believed that I was unworthy of friendship or love. I believed that there was no hope that my life would change. I have heard these two beliefs expressed over the years by the young people with whom I have worked and have done my best to help youth transcend these two self-defeating beliefs, as I have myself. What worked for me? To the best of my memory, the most important positive influences in my childhood were the adults who showed an interest in me—who spent time with me, noticed what I was doing right, and showed by their attention, words, and actions that they saw me as having value. My parents did that, yet for me that was not enough. I remember a neighbor who took me for walks with his children and noticed that I saw birds and salamanders and trees. I remember my elementary school librarian, who let me stay in at recess to help her shelve books and talk about literature. Though I have forgotten her name, I have always felt that she knew that she was protecting me. I remember my eighth grade teacher, Carol Anderson, who let me help her set up science experiments and told me positive things about my actions. I remember Ben Alper, the 30-year mentor I described previously, who found ways to show me that my actions and ideas and curiosity had value. I remember Edith Busse, my creative writing teacher in high school, who talked to me about my stories and poems in a way that made her respect clear. What helped me was the time and caring expressed by adults. In addition, I chose to pursue music, to involve myself in service and justice activities, and to immerse myself in the outdoors. I have been blessed in my family and friends.

I want to address one more question in this preface: How did my childhood history affect my life path? I might have become a microbiologist or an engineer or a musician if I had followed the paths of things I loved as a child. The clarity of science, in which inquiry and learning and evidence mean everything, still appeals to me greatly. The research we will describe in this book is my first venture into real science of that kind, and I am grateful to Charisse for helping me find a path into those youthful dreams after all these decades. I still love music and pursue it with my whole heart. Yet my difficult childhood and my gratitude to the adults who turned me from disaster to hope moved my path toward fighting for social justice and working to improve the lives of young people. I just retired after 42 years' work, first as a child and family therapist and then as a school counselor. I continue to support schools and educators in their efforts to improve the lives of young people. I have found this work deeply fulfilling and am glad that I followed this life path. Perhaps my social isolation as a child has led me to value my current family and friendships and community more deeply than I would otherwise. My experience echoes what my friend and esteemed colleague Linda Sanford (2005) found in the research for her wonderful book *Strong at the Broken Places: Building Resiliency in Survivors of Trauma.* As she teaches us, survivors of emotional trauma can be strengthened. That strength comes not from the trauma but from the support we receive as we work to overcome it.

CHARISSE'S STORY

"The only whole heart is a broken heart," says Mitch Albom in his 2009 book, *Have a Little Faith*. My passion for work in bullying prevention was and continues to be ignited by broken hearts but, importantly, continues to be fueled by hope: a hope that surpasses the pessimism that surrounds too many of our youth and a hope rooted in the human spirit and supported by science.

My journey into this work began like that of so many others, as a response to broken hearts—the broken hearts of thousands of children and youth, the broken hearts of my friends, the broken hearts of my siblings, and last, but not least, my own broken heart. Each of us has a story to tell—a story that cuts across age, gender, race, and any other demographic—that if we are courageous enough to tell, will connect us to one another and, if we are lucky, over time will heal us.

I grew up in a family probably not that different from your own, a family with two loving parents, two sisters and two brothers. Our family valued hard work and education, kindness and compassion. What was different about my family was that both of my sisters and one of my brothers were born with a genetic disorder called Marfan syndrome. Marfans, as it is sometimes referred to, is a connective tissue disorder that affects the heart, bones, tendons, cartilage, eyes, skin, and lungs, among other systems. Although this genetic disorder varies in symptomology, to the naked eye, one thing is clear—many children affected by Marfan syndrome look different. For example, children affected by Marfan syndrome typically have a long narrow face with very long legs and arms. They are often very tall, with a curved spine. Most are nearsighted. Looking different in a culture that values physical appearance above all else can be traumatic.

What this translated to me as a child was simple: I had a front row seat to watch relentless, heart-wrenching peer mistreatment on a regular basis. But these were not just any peers being mistreated: These were my siblings. Children who witness mistreatment between adults experience negative effects (e.g., Cummings & Davies, 1994). We now know that bearing witness to peer mistreatment also causes harm (Janosz, Archambault, Pagani, Pascal, Morin, & Bowen, 2008).

Although all my siblings have significantly influenced me over the years, I want to take a moment to introduce you to the sister closest in age to me, my sister Cindy. Cindy was thinner than most kids our age, had unusually long limbs and a curved spine, and wore thick glasses. Looking different was enough to make a child a target of mistreatment 30 years ago. (By the way, is it any different today? Are kids who look different because of disabilities or body weight targeted more than kids who do not look different? We will look at this question later on in the book as we dig deeper into the patterns of peer mistreatment.) Cindy was a year older than me, and as a result we shared most things, whether we liked it or not. We shared a bedroom, we shared a closet, and we shared our clothes. We even shared our friends. But what I never considered until my adult years was that I also shared her pain. Of course, that is not to say that I could ever know or feel the full depth of her pain. Cindy endured more grief and loss during her childhood and adolescence than I could ever imagine. My earliest memories of Cindy take place on the school bus.

I have vivid memories of getting on the bus in the morning. I was in third grade; Cindy was in fourth grade (which at the time seemed so much older). I remember the feeling in my stomach when it started. Cindy would get on the bus and look around for a seat. Inevitably, one of the boys would grab one of her books (we didn't use backpacks then) and start playing a "friendly" game of catch with his friends. At first, Cindy tried to get her book back. When it became obvious it wasn't going to happen, she turned her efforts toward trying to find a place on the bus to sit down and escape the public ridicule. Although the girls weren't as verbal as the boys, they were just as mean-spirited. When she would try to sit down next to a girl, the girl would inevitably slide her books over and say "saved." Cindy continued on to the next seat. You may wonder what the bus driver was doing while all this was going on. Certainly, he must have addressed the situation and supported Cindy in some way. No! The bus driver was preoccupied with getting everyone to sit down before he could move the bus. He was also yelling at Cindy. He was yelling, "Sit down!"

My response . . .

I imagine you are wondering what my response was. What did I do? Did I stand up for my sister? Did I tell the bus driver? Did I tell a teacher? Did I tell an adult at home? Surprisingly, my response over 30 years ago was not very different from the responses of thousands of children and adolescents recently surveyed in our Youth Voice Project. I watched. I listened. I sat quietly. And I did nothing . . . but pray for it to stop. You're probably thinking that certainly things must have changed over the past 30 years. Have they? This is one of the golden questions we will unpack as we delve into children's responses to peer mistreatment. What does the bystander do? What bystander actions actually help to support the mistreated child and reduce associated trauma?

Although the details changed, I was privy to this sort of mistreatment day after day. And because we shared a bedroom, I was also privy to Cindy's tears at night. I heard Cindy's tears, loud and clear, but remained frozen in my bed, lying just a few feet away from her. I didn't get up and comfort her. I didn't even provide encouraging words. I just lay there, pretending I didn't hear her, hoping she would soon fall asleep, praying for someone to take away her pain. I was not courageous. I was a coward: too afraid to do anything, too heavy with grief to reach out. After having many years to process this, I have often thought about what would have made a difference. What did I need to be able to do to support my sister?

What I needed . . .

I realize now that what I needed was for someone to talk with me and encourage me to do something, to remind me that I could make a difference and help Cindy feel better. I needed someone to tell me that I didn't have to make the mistreatment stop to help my sister. I needed to hear that encouraging and kind words, although seemingly insignificant, were enough to make a difference. I could have acknowledged the painful treatment my sister was receiving, checked in with her, listened to her, reminded her that I loved her and that I was sorry she was going through this. Unfortunately, no one helped me to see this. How could they? No one knew. I never told anyone. We grew up paralyzed in a world of silence, a world where pain was not discussed and sorrows were not shared. Nobody talked about it, including

Cindy and me. We never even acknowledged the mistreatment. It was too hard—too painful. You will hear throughout this book the importance of building children's self-efficacy: moving them from feelings of helplessness and silence to feelings of empowerment and choice. We believe that building self-efficacy is important for all children. Self-efficacy is needed for those children who are directly mistreated as well as for those children who bear witness to the mistreatment.

Cindy's story ended early. Unfortunately, she died unexpectedly at a young age. In the end, I was never able to tell her how sorry I was for not supporting her. I supported her in other ways, but I was never able to confront the pain around her mistreatment. Today, I have dedicated my life to protecting children and adolescents from peer mistreatment and to instilling confidence and self-efficacy in witnesses so that they are able to support others who are hurting.

Here's where the hope comes in . . .

Unlike genetic disorders or terrorist threats—things we have no control over—we do have control over peer mistreatment and its associated harm. As many scholars have wisely reminded us, the major threats facing our children and youth are no longer rooted in disease. Instead, the major threats facing them are rooted in relationships. And it is to those relationships that dedicate the pages of this book.

Bridges change the landscape of the culture. Our challenge in changing the culture starts with each of us, whether you work with children and teenagers or are a single adult. We all have a responsibility to intentionally build bridges, to provide others with messages about how to treat people and about what kinds of behavior we are and are not willing to tolerate. I am now the parent of two beautiful children. You may wonder what I want for my children. I want them to actively support others who are hurting. I want them to use their words to build others up instead of tear them down. I want them to be able to seek out support when they are hurting and not suffer in silence. But for those things to happen, Stan and I are convinced we need to create a different kind of culture—a culture of acceptance and inclusion, where it is safe to talk about feelings honestly, without judgment or fear.

We do know that change in this direction can be sustained only by addressing our belief systems and by challenging ourselves to think about which kinds of behaviors and attitudes we are willing to tolerate and which kinds we are not. We do know that change is often uncomfortable and difficult—that we tend to resist change but that gradually change can become the new norm. We do know that change starts with each one of us. And, most important, we do know that positive change can happen.

Acknowledgments

We to express our gratitude to the many educators, counselors, and administrators who made time in their difficult school schedules for students to take our survey. We also want to thank Julia McLeod for her invaluable editing and organizational work on this book and acknowledge the dedication and efforts of the following undergraduate students at Penn State Erie, The Behrend College:

We want to affirm and thank all the dedicated educators who do so much for our youth and express gratitude to the following undergraduate students at Penn State Erie, The Behrend College, for their time and dedication to the project:

Kimberly Cook	Paige Robertson
Alyson Eagle	Emily Sherry
James Heubel	Jennifer Slane
Denise Hillen	Jaclyn Stottlemyer
Janice Jerome	Danielle Wilson
Carl Kallgren IV	Abby Zehe

Our admiration and thanks go to all adults and peers who help mistreated and socially isolated young people build hope, connection, and resiliency. Most important of all, though, are the contributions of the vast numbers of students who put so much time and effort into answering the questions on our survey. Without their voices, there would be no book.

INTRODUCTION

Preventing Bullying and Preventing Harm

Many of us in education chose our career path because of the positive impact school had on our own lives. That impact is exemplified by a past student at the James Bean Elementary School in Sidney, Maine, where Stan worked as a school counselor for 12 years. At the end of her last year at the Bean School, this young person reflected on her childhood. Her life at home had been difficult in many ways, including several incidents of abuse and an overall pattern of emotional neglect. Yet at age 12 she was a confident individual with a web of friendships and a strong mastery drive. She frequently did kind things for others. When Stan asked her how she had made her life so positive, she thought for a while and responded, "I take the way school is . . . home with me." Schools can be a sanctuary, a springboard, and a positive beginning for life.

This book highlights the results of the Youth Voice Project, an extensive survey of youth from 31 schools across the United States. Through these pages, you will discover the heart of our nation's youth. As we present their stories, don't be surprised to hear part of your own story embedded in their words. In reading their stories, it is our hope that you will be inspired to remember the reason you chose to work with children and adolescents in the first place—to change lives, one child at a time. We hope that adults and youth can use what we've learned to make life better for all.

This book is not about what adults think might help to address peer mistreatment. Instead, this book represents the voices of youth, some of whom have been mistreated by their peers. We are concerned that too much work in this field has focused on adults telling youth what bullying is and what to do to address bullying behavior. In reality, youth are the primary experts on what is happening at school and on what works best to address peer mistreatment. Through the survey, we seek to bring youth into a dialogue as equal partners with adult educators and researchers. We see authentic youth involvement as key to success in bullying prevention.

Our survey results are both encouraging and disturbing. We are convinced that to protect our children we need a cultural change. In order to raise happy, healthy, confident, caring children, we need a culture where mean-spirited behavior is no longer tolerated, even in the name of friendship or "just joking around." We need a culture where we all look out for one another—old and young, popular and unpopular. We need to build a culture where we take the time to truly listen to one another. We need to develop a culture where people are responsible for their behavior and are trained to show others they are sorry instead of merely saying they are sorry. We need a culture where it is safe to talk about feelings honestly and without judgment or fear.

We believe it is possible to decide together to change the social climate of our schools, sports teams, buses, hallways, neighborhoods, and homes. Change is not going to happen by itself; rather, it needs to be intentional on all levels. Change requires us to address our belief systems and think about which behaviors and attitudes we are willing to tolerate and which we are not willing to tolerate. We know that change is often uncomfortable and difficult, but a more inclusive environment can gradually become the new normal. We invite parents to explore our research as well, both as advocates for effective interventions in schools and to use what we have learned to give support to their own children who may be mistreated.

Change starts with each of us, but we need to agree on our goals. During our combined 23 years of work in bullying prevention, we have done a lot of thinking and talking with teachers, administrators, trainers, and students. On top of this experience, we have analyzed the thousands of youth responses to the Youth Voice Project survey.

There is some good news: The field of bullying prevention has improved in several key ways since the 1950s. We take this issue much more seriously now and see adults as responsible for taking positive action. There are national and local conversations about how to protect young people from the trauma of peer mistreatment and ostracism. Youth are much less likely to be told, "Don't let it bother you. Kids are mean sometimes."

But we still need change. Instead of focusing primarily on identifying and punishing the "bullies," we should be looking at ways to build inclusive, fair, and respectful school cultures. This shift toward a focus on school culture started with the important work of researchers and visionaries including Dan Olweus (1993), Peter Smith (Smith, Mortia, Junger-Tas, Olweus, Catalano, & Slee, 1999), Dorothea Ross (2003), and many others. We have also turned toward a greater focus on the powerful role of youth bystanders. It is clear that actions of inclusion and emotional support by young people's peers are a positive force for good.

It is time to abandon the idea that mistreated youth somehow caused their own mistreatment by being passive or provocative. Linked to this idea is the commonly expressed idea that if mistreated youth would only assert themselves or not show that they are bothered by negative actions or walk away or tell the mistreater how they feel, the mistreatment would stop. These actions, on average, were not helpful for the mistreated students who participated in the Youth Voice Project. We are concerned that such advice can lead mistreated youth to blame themselves for what has been done to them and thus to accept the negative opinions expressed by their tormentors.

We have come to believe that the words we have used to describe peer mistreatment—*bullying, bullies,* and *victims*—may do more harm than good. Adults and youth have been taught to identify bullying as behavior that is intended to harm, cuts across a power differential, and is repeated. In our work with youth and educators within the United States and around the world, we have heard many accounts of harmful peer actions that were ignored because the adult observing them knew that the peer "didn't mean any harm." We have heard young people minimize the impact of their own hurtful actions because they aren't "bullies" and didn't intend to hurt. Regardless of intent or power differential, mean or cruel behavior often causes harm, and bullying as conventionally defined is a subset of mean or cruel behavior. Harm can be done by the actions of a close friend or in the context of an isolated event. Harm can be done even if the person saying or doing something is truly just joking, with no intent to harm. When deciding how to respond to a behavior, we can be more effective if we look at one variable only: the potential for harm inherent in that action.

Use of the term *bullying* encourages people to look for "bullies" rather than to look for mean behaviors that anyone may choose and that can do harm no matter who uses them. We should talk about what an individual does, not who the person is. For those reasons, we will use the words *peer mistreatment* instead of the word *bullying* throughout this book. We will continue to use the phrase *bullying prevention* at times for clarity.

Too often in this work, we want to find simple answers to complex problems. We want to highlight robust patterns to explain all students' behavior. In reality, we know that life is not simple. Though we will compare the helpfulness of actions that mistreated youth, their peers, and adults can take, we need to remember that one size does not fit all. Knowing that some actions work better than others can serve as a guide for us; however, we need to be patient and willing to look at complex answers to complex issues. In real life, we need to consider many different ways to solve problems. Similarly, we need to consider many different variables as we seek to reduce peer mistreatment and its associated harm. That said, the large amount of data generated by the survey is a major strength of this book. We are basing our recommendations on what thousands of students told us. Patterns of students' responses can guide us in our work.

Our work has led us to identify six primary goals in handling peer mistreatment:

- First, we should strive to reduce the frequency of thoughtless, mean actions carried out by youth who do not intend to harm others but who may be imitating negative social modeling and/or are striving to fit in with their peers. This reduction can be accomplished through the use of consistent rules and small, escalating consequences. We can also build awareness of the effects of mean actions. We can help youth shape positive peer norms.

- Second, we should seek to reduce the frequency of mean actions committed by youth who have deficits in conscience, self-control, or empathy. Helping these young people change often involves repeated, patient skill instruction combined with the use of small consequences. We should also help mistreating youth who have a history of trauma to build new patterns of behavior as we help them heal from traumatic events.

- Third, we should reduce the frequency of mean behavior by a very small group of young people who truly enjoy hurting others. Doing so often requires mobilizing significant resources over time. However, interventions with this group justify the use of these resources because effects these young people's behaviors are likely to have on themselves and on others are severe.

- Fourth, we should build cognitive and emotional resiliency in all youth to prepare them to cope with others' negative actions and with the inevitable losses and disappointments of life. All youth need to learn emotional awareness, emotional self-care, when and how to seek help, and cognitive skills to reduce self-blame and trauma.

- Fifth, we should build connectedness and relationships for all within the school community so no one has to go through difficult times alone. A large body of research shows that youth who have positive connections with adults outside the family become more resilient—that is, they are less likely to be traumatized by negative events. In addition, developing research on the effects of social isolation and ostracism suggests that social isolation at school is uniquely damaging and that connections with both peers and adults are a key element in preventing harm.

- Sixth, we should strengthen our community's responses to mistreatment and trauma, including in our work efforts to recruit and encourage youth who will mentor, support, and listen to mistreated youth.

Combating peer mistreatment is not just about stopping mean and cruel behavior. We can make a dent in the problem by enforcing consistent discipline and helping young people learn to be kinder. Given human nature, this effort will never be 100 percent successful. Thus, our interventions must *also* focus on reducing the harm that ensues from peer mistreatment. This book therefore focuses on the latter three goals: promoting resiliency, building connections, and developing adult and peer support for mistreated youth. In addition to pursuing these three goals, schools should do everything in their power to reduce the frequency and intensity of potentially hurtful peer actions. For more information on school discipline interventions, we encourage you to read Stan's book *Schools Where Everyone Belongs* (Davis, 2007b). For more information and some additional material that did not find its way into this book, visit the Youth Voice Project website (www.youthvoiceproject.com).

CHAPTER 1

The Youth Voice Project: Study Rationale and Methodology

The goal is to turn data into information, and information into insight.

—Carly Fiorina, former CEO of Hewlett-Packard

To this point, researchers have studied several facets of peer mistreatment, including but not limited to prevalence (e.g., Nansel et al., 2001), related somatic complaints (e.g., Nixon, Linkie, Coleman, & Fitch, 2011), correlated psychological outcomes (e.g., Prinstein, Boergers, & Vernberg, 2001), and gender differences (for a review, see Card, Stucky, Sawalani, & Little, 2008). However, to our knowledge, the Youth Voice Project is the first large scale national research effort to study the effects of specific actions taken by mistreated youth, by adults at school, and by these youths' peers. Before now, limited research has focused on hypothetical scenarios highlighting targets' strategies to stop the bullying, without considering peer and adult actions and often without considering grade level and gender effects. Unless we invite students to contribute their unique perspectives and real-world experience to this conversation, we cannot know what truly helps or hurts mistreated students.

A primary goal of the Youth Voice Project has been to investigate and understand the ways adults and peers can reduce the harm caused by peer mistreatment. To do this, we explored the role mistreated students, peers, and adults play in the healing process. We asked mistreated students which of their own actions, their peers' actions, and adults' actions made things better for them and which made things worse. We also explored how severe peer mistreatment affected students and tried to tease out which factors influenced their related trauma levels. We asked about students' feelings of school connection and looked at the potential impact that connection had on their trauma levels. Another goal of the study has been to assess equity in our schools. We analyzed peer mistreatment, trauma, and adult and peer actions by subgroup to learn more about the experiences of different demographic groups in our schools.

To make this book as reader friendly as possible, we have chosen not to include detailed statistics, including probability levels. To stay true to the science, however, any differences described in this book are significant at the accepted probability level ($p < .05$).*

WHO TOOK PART IN THE YOUTH VOICE PROJECT?

A total of 13,177 students from across the United States participated in the study. Overall, 31 schools in 12 states participated. The students ranged in age from 11 to 19. Ten percent represented elementary school (fifth grade), 57 percent represented middle school (sixth through eighth grades), and 33 percent represented high school (ninth through twelfth grades). Half were female, and half were male. The sample consisted of 50 percent White, 14 percent Hispanic American, 8 percent African American, 7 percent Multiracial, 4 percent Asian American, 3 percent Native American, and 14 percent other race or unreported. Thirty-one percent of students received reduced or free hot lunches at school or were eligible for free or reduced lunch. Seven percent of the youth reported having a physical disability, and 8 percent reported getting help from special education.

Schools heard about the study through email or word of mouth and through announcements in organizational newsletters. All schools who expressed interest were allowed to participate. Anonymous online questionnaires were administered to students on computers at school in the fall of 2010. Each participating school made an effort to survey all its students, except for youth whose parents or guardians opted out of the survey. The number of students whose parents or guardians chose to opt out was negligible. In the survey, students were told that all responses would be kept confidential and that their participation was completely voluntary. Questionnaires took approximately 45 minutes to complete, and teachers were present to provide assistance with reading and technology if needed. The study was approved by the institutional review board at Penn State University.

SURVEY QUESTIONS

We worked with colleagues and youth across the United States to brainstorm and refine survey questions. In the end, we decided on 45 questions: a total of 33 multiple choice questions and 12 open-ended text questions. (Please see the appendix for the full survey.) In this book, we will not analyze the entire survey; however, we include the most relevant questions here.

Demographics

We gathered demographic data, including age, gender, grade level, racial or cultural background, socioeconomic status, and whether or not students had physical disabilities or received help from special education.

---

*For more details about the Youth Voice Project statistical analyses, please email Charisse Nixon at cln5@psu.edu.

School connection

We asked three questions to gauge students' feelings of connectedness to school:

- I feel like I am part of this school.
  - ○ NO!
  - ○ No
  - ○ Unsure
  - ○ Yes
  - ○ YES!

- I feel valued and respected at school.
  - ○ NO!
  - ○ No
  - ○ Unsure
  - ○ Yes
  - ○ YES!

- I feel close to adults at my school.
  - ○ NO!
  - ○ No
  - ○ Unsure
  - ○ Yes
  - ○ YES!

Prevalence of peer mistreatment

We assessed the prevalence of peer mistreatment by asking students how often in the last month they were the target of relational or physical peer mistreatment:

- In the past month, how often have students at your school hurt you emotionally or excluded you?
  - ○ Every day
  - ○ Once a week
  - ○ Two or three times a month
  - ○ One time
  - ○ Never

- In the past month, how often have students at your school threatened to hurt you or hurt you physically?
  - ○ Every day
  - ○ Once a week

○ Two or three times a month

○ One time

○ Never

Following procedures used in past work (Olweus, 1993, 1997; Solberg & Olweus, 2003), we classified students as mistreated if they reported relational and/or physical mistreatment by their peers at least twice a month or more in the previous month. Students classified as mistreated were directed to a series of questions focusing on what actions they, adults, and peers took in response to their peer mistreatment. The remaining students were directed to an alternative survey about their observations and experiences as bystanders.

Focus of mistreatment

We asked participants about the focus of the peer mistreatment:

- Did the people who hurt you focus on any of these issues? You may click more than one option. Please do not include any names.

  ○ Race

  ○ Looks

  ○ Gender or gender expression

  ○ Sexual orientation

  ○ Religion

  ○ Family income

  ○ Body shape

  ○ Disability

  ○ Other (please specify)

Perceived trauma

Knowing that not all youth are affected in the same way by peer mistreatment, we wanted to assess students' levels of perceived trauma as it related to their experiences with peer mistreatment. We asked students about the impact of their peer mistreatment:

- How severe was the impact of what they did on you?

  ○ Mild: What they did bothered me only a little.

  ○ Moderate: It bothered me quite a bit.

  ○ Severe: I had or have trouble eating, sleeping, or enjoying myself because of what happened to me.

  ○ Very severe: I felt or feel unsafe and threatened because of what happened to me.

Self-actions

We also asked mistreated youth to indicate what they did when they were mistreated and what happened after they did that. Throughout the book, we call these *self-actions.*

- Did you do any of these things about what was done to you? What helped? Please click one option for each action.

	I didn't do this	I did it and things got worse	I did it and nothing changed	I did it and things got better
Pretended it didn't bother me.	○	○	○	○
Reminded myself that what they are doing is not my fault and that THEY are the ones who are doing something wrong.	○	○	○	○
Made plans to get back at them or fight them.	○	○	○	○
Hit them or fought them.	○	○	○	○
Told the person or people to stop.	○	○	○	○
Did nothing.	○	○	○	○
Told the person or people how I felt about what they were doing.	○	○	○	○
Walked away.	○	○	○	○
Told an adult at school.	○	○	○	○
Told an adult at home.	○	○	○	○
Told a friend(s).	○	○	○	○
Made a joke about it.	○	○	○	○

Other (What else did you do and how much did it help?)

Adult actions

We asked mistreated students what adults did in response to their mistreatment and what resulted from their action. Throughout the book, we call these *adult actions.*

- What did adults at school do about what was done to you? What happened when they did those things? Please click one option for each action.

	Adults didn't do this	Adults did this and things got worse	Adults did this and there was no change	Adults did this and things got better
Gave me advice.	○	○	○	○
Listened to me.	○	○	○	○
Ignored what was going on.	○	○	○	○
Told me to solve the problem myself.	○	○	○	○
Told me to stop tattling.	○	○	○	○
Told me that if I acted differently this wouldn't happen to me.	○	○	○	○
Said they would talk with the other student or students.	○	○	○	○
Sat down with me and the other student or students together.	○	○	○	○
Used punishments for the other student(s).	○	○	○	○
Checked in with me afterwards to see if the behavior stopped.	○	○	○	○
Kept up increased adult supervision for some time.	○	○	○	○
Talked with the whole class or school about the behavior.	○	○	○	○
Brought in a speaker to talk with the whole class or school about the behavior.	○	○	○	○
Talked about the behavior in class more than once.	○	○	○	○

Other (What else did adults do and how much did it help?)

Peer actions

We asked mistreated students what peers did in response to their mistreatment and what resulted from their action. Throughout the book, we call these responses *peer actions.*

- What did other students do about what was done to you? What happened when they did that? Please click one option for each action.

	No one did this	Other students did this and things got worse	Other students did this and things didn't change	Other students did this and things got better
Told the person to stop in a mean or angry way.	○	○	○	○
Listened to me.	○	○	○	○
Asked the person to stop being mean to me in a friendly way.	○	○	○	○
Ignored what was going on.	○	○	○	○
Spent time with me, sat with me, or hung out with me.	○	○	○	○
Gave me advice about what I should do.	○	○	○	○
Blamed me for what was happening.	○	○	○	○
Made fun of me for asking for help or for being treated badly.	○	○	○	○
Called me at home to encourage me.	○	○	○	○
Talked to me at school to encourage me.	○	○	○	○
Told an adult.	○	○	○	○
Helped me tell an adult.	○	○	○	○
Helped me get away from situations where the behavior was going on.	○	○	○	○
Distracted the people who were treating me badly.	○	○	○	○

Other (What else did other students do and how much did it help?)

To compare and contrast self-, adult, and peer actions, we calculated a helpfulness score for each action. We gave 1 point to the action when a student reported that things got better, 0 points to the action when a student reported that nothing changed, and negative 1 point to the action when a student reported that things got worse. Then we divided the total number of points for each action by the number of students who had used or experienced that action.

Open-ended questions

In addition to looking at quantitative data, we also wanted to hear about young people's experiences in their own words. We asked all youth who reported repeated mistreatment (a total of nearly 3,000) a series of open-ended text questions to gather more information about their experiences:

- If you feel comfortable, please describe what happened to you. Because this is a confidential survey, please also tell an adult you trust at school about what happened if you have not already done that. Please do not include any names.

  Overall, what did you do that helped you the most?

  What happened when you did that?

  What else do you wish you had done?

  Overall, what did adults do that helped the most?

  What happened when they did that?

  What else do you wish adults had done?

  Overall, what did other students do that helped the most?

  What happened when they did that?

  What else do you wish other students had done?

  What have you done to help another student be safe or have friends at school? Again, because this survey is confidential, please do NOT include any names. Thanks!

  What have you done to help another student be safe or have friends at school? Again, because this survey is confidential, please do NOT include any names. Thanks!

  What happened when you did that?

CHAPTER 2

Characteristics and Impact of Peer Mistreatment

Each of us can practice rights ourselves, treating each other without discrimination, respecting each other's dignity and rights.

—*Carol Bellamy, former director of UNICEF*

More than one-fourth of students who participated in the Youth Voice Project reported that they were mistreated physically or relationally at least twice a month or more in the past month, a finding consistent with that of other studies (e.g., Nansel et al., 2001; Solberg & Olweus, 2003). That's approximately 3,000 students.

WERE THERE DIFFERENCES IN GRADE LEVEL?

Past research has shown that physical aggression peaks in young childhood, whereas relational aggression peaks in early adolescence (Bjorkqvist, Lagerspetz, & Kaukiainen, 1992; Scheithauer, Hayer, Petermann, & Jugert 2006). Consistent with past work, we found that students in grades 5 through 12 reported more relational mistreatment than physical mistreatment. In fact, twice as many students reported relational mistreatment as reported physical mistreatment (see Table 2.1).

WERE THERE DIFFERENCES IN GENDER?

There were no gender differences in the rate of relational mistreatment. Males and females at all grade levels were equally likely to report experiencing relational mistreatment. However, when it came to physical mistreatment, as expected, males reported a higher rate than females. Although females did not experience as much physical mistreatment as males, they did experience varying levels of physical mistreatment across grade level. For example, females experienced more physical mistreatment in elementary school than in middle and high school, whereas males experienced a similar amount of physical mistreatment across all grade levels (see Table 2.2).

Past research has shown that relational mistreatment, including exclusion, can have a significant negative impact on youth. Kip Williams (2001) conducted a series of laboratory studies on face-to-face ostracism and Internet exclusion. He

Table 2.1: Overall rates of physical and relational mistreatment

	Physical mistreatment	Relational mistreatment
Never	76%	50%
One time	13%	24%
Two or three times a month	4%	11%
Once a week	3%	8%
Every day	4%	7%

found that being exposed to social exclusion for only five minutes reduced college students' feelings of belongingness, control, self-esteem, and meaningful existence. Clearly, many students are being ostracized for more than five minutes. Though many people dismiss exclusion as being "part of growing up," a body of empirical work now informs us that social exclusion (face to face or via the Internet) threatens children's well-being and, as a result, must be taken seriously.

WHAT WAS THE FOCUS OF THE MISTREATMENT?

Students were asked to indicate what issues the people mistreating them focused on, as well as to describe what happened to them in their own words. Youth responded that mistreatment most commonly focused on looks and body shape (see Table 2.3).

Of the mistreated students, more than 1,000 wrote brief text descriptions of what happened to them. In reading through the text responses, some patterns emerged. First, much of the mistreatment focused on students' differences. Youth reported mistreatment focusing on height, body shape, the way they talked, and other ways in which they were different. Second, as many other writers have discussed (e.g., Rivers, 2001), a significant amount of mistreatment focused on enforcing narrow gender norms and on using the words *gay* or *lesbian* as insults, whether or not the person being called those names was in fact gay or lesbian. Many youth reported that this form of mistreatment interfered with their establishing and maintaining meaningful friendships.

Table 2.2: Grade level and gender comparison for students who were mistreated physically and relationally by their peers at least twice a month in the past month

	Physical mistreatment		Relational mistreatment	
	Females	Males	Females	Males
Overall	.87	1.65	2.65	2.58
Elementary school	1.15	1.64	2.74	2.69
Middle school	.88	1.58	2.64	2.59
High school	.78	1.79	2.62	2.58

Note: Every day=4, Once a week=3, Two or three times a month=2, One time=1, Never=0

Table 2.3: Affirmative responses to the question "Did the people who hurt you focus on any of these issues?"

	Percentage of students indicating that mistreatment focused on this issue
Looks	48%
Body shape	30%
Race	14%
Gender or gender expression	11%
Sexual orientation	11%
Religion	9%
Family income	9%
Disability	9%

YOUTH VOICES

Here are some examples from students' text descriptions of their mistreatment:

"i was called a creeper and that I'm a no one and have no friends."

"I was called "guppy" because they said I have big eyes like a guppy fish:("

"there are a couple of people last year, who would make fun of me because of my being a little over-weight body type, and they would constantly pick on me, and talk about me behind my back, but this year, i feel she is kind of doing it, because when i was walking from my bus stop, she started to yell that im fat, and i don't belong on this planet, but when im at school, she'll smile at me, and talk to me once in a while like nothings happened. and i don't get it. i think when she's around me, she's nice, and when she's not, she constantly talks about me . . . i just want it to stop . . . and for people to like me the way i am."

"said that i was uncool because of the food i bring to school and my clothing"

"I was made fun of for not being a virgin. And rumors were spread that I had an std and i was a slut."

"a boy told me that i cry like a girl and punched me on the arm."

"i was called ugly and people were spreading rumors around that i was a lesbian and made out with a girl, and none of that is true."

"he started to spread a rumor that I looked up men's balls on the internet. He then started to call me a gay faggot every time he saw me."

"well, alot of people have called me gay because of how i act."

"I was called a sped and stupid many times by girls at my school."

"my nickname is waddles and everybody calls me that and a rumor went around that im nothing and poor."

"i was called a stupid jew and told to go do things like to go to hell, and go burn in a oven happened almost every day when i was in middle school and I'm worried it will happen in high school unless someone does something about it."

"a frie3nd i[s] blaming me and telling rumors about me and is making me sad and its like they're turning everybody against me."

WHO DID AND DID NOT EXPERIENCE TRAUMA?

Because stopping 100 percent of peer mistreatment is an unrealistic goal, in addition to understanding the nature of peer mistreatment, we also wanted to find out how to reduce the trauma. As described earlier, to answer this question we asked mistreated youth how deeply they were emotionally affected by what was done to them. Students chose from the following four options:

- Mild: What they did bothered me only a little.
- Moderate: It bothered me quite a bit.
- Severe: I had or have trouble eating, sleeping, or enjoying myself because of what happened to me.
- Very severe: I felt or feel unsafe and threatened because of what happened to me.

As shown in Tables 2.4 through 2.6, our data show that some students who were repeatedly mistreated experienced moderate to very severe trauma and others experienced only mild trauma. According to past work, children's response to stressors depends on several factors, including individual factors such as gender and age, the frequency of mistreatment, and school-related variables (Compas, Connor-Smith, Saltzman, Thomsen, & Wadsworth, 2001; Compas, Malcarne, & Fondacaro, 1988; Griffith, Dubow, & Ippolito, 2000).

We looked for connections between how much trauma (mild or moderate to very severe) mistreated students experienced and the frequency of their mistreatment, by grade level and gender. As shown in Table 2.4, youth reported that relational mistreatment hurt as much as physical mistreatment did.

As Table 2.5 indicates, younger students were more likely than older students to report moderate to very severe trauma from peer mistreatment. More than three-quarters of mistreated elementary school students reported moderate to very severe trauma, compared to less than one-half of high school students. More females than males reported moderate to very severe trauma from being mistreated by their peers (see Table 2.6). Clearly, we needed to look more deeply for the factors that influence students' trauma levels.

When we compared the text descriptions of mistreatment of those who experienced moderate to very severe trauma with the descriptions of those who experienced mild trauma, we found no obvious pattern. Other factors beside the words

Table 2.4: Prevalence of types of mistreatment and trauma levels

	Mild trauma (N=1,351)	Moderate to very severe trauma (N=1,578)
Physical mistreatment (twice a month or more in the past month)	41%	59%
Relational mistreatment (twice a month or more in the past month)	44%	56%

Table 2.5: Grade and trauma levels

	Mild trauma (N=1,351)	Moderate to very severe trauma (N=1,578)
Elementary school	22%	78%
Middle school	46%	54%
High school	55%	45%

said clearly also influence trauma levels. Take a look at the following lists of behaviors and try to distinguish which list was written by each group (i.e., those reporting no or mild trauma versus those reporting moderate to very severe trauma).

Group A

"I can barely play anything at recess because people exclude me a lot."

"A friend told my secrets that I thought she would keep private."

"Rumors were started about me."

"I was called 'guppy' because they said I have big eyes like a guppy fish:("

"a girl who i used to hang out with told everyone that I was a bad person and that i was rude."

"at lunch a girl calls me fat and ugly."

"making fun of me because i don't have a boy friend and not good looking."

"said that i was uncool because of the food i bring to school and my clothing."

Group B

"im kinda short and made fun of and people tend to knock me down in the hallways or friends dont relize how fragile i am."

"I was made fun of by boys in my class that i was ugly and fat."

"A girl in 7th grade threatens to beat me up if they see me outside of the school one day."

"People call me a whore and fire crotch. And its mean."

"i was punched in the back and chest by a female student."

"People talked about my body shape and used it to hurt me."

Table 2.6: Gender and trauma levels

	Mild trauma (N=1,351)	Moderate to very severe trauma (N=1,578)
Females	40%	60%
Males	53%	47%

"I just got excluded and it hurt my feelings."

"this girl was telling lies to my friends to try to make them stop liking me and people are scared of her so they do it otherwise she's mean to them."

Group A reported moderate to very severe trauma following the peer mistreatment. Group B reported mild trauma. Some may argue that the youth in group B could have become habituated to the mistreatment. In reading the text narratives, however, we found very few accounts that confirmed that idea. Instead, youth often identified protective factors that lessened the impact of others' negative actions on them. We will discuss these protective factors throughout this book.

CHAPTER 3

School Connection

Humans are hardwired to form relationships.

—*Commission on Children at Risk*

All humans are biologically wired to seek connections to other people and to moral and spiritual meaning, according to a report from a group of 33 pediatricians, research scientists, and mental health and youth service professionals (Commission on Children at Risk, 2003). This report comes on the heels of similar assertions by many prominent scholars, including the late Peter Benson, CEO of the Search Institute in Minneapolis. Benson spent his career helping educators, researchers, and caring adults focus on the positive aspects of youth development, an approach that highlighted what he termed *developmental assets* (Scales & Roehlkepartain, 2012).

Social psychologists Roy Baumeister and Mark Leary (1995) describe the need to make connections, belong, and be accepted by others as a basic motivational need that drives behavior. Kip Williams (1997, 2001) asserts that being ostracized threatens one's sense of belongingness, control, perceived self-esteem, and meaningful existence. Michael Resnick and his colleagues (Resnick et al., 1997) surveyed more than 12,000 youth to find out what protects kids from emotional distress, suicidal thoughts and behaviors, violence, substance abuse, and sexual behaviors. Results from their study showed that family connectedness and perceived school connectedness were protective against nearly every risk factor identified among the youth studied.

The Wingspread Declaration on School Connections (Blum & Libbey, 2004) lays out some of the arguments for enhancing students' connection to school:

> Student success can be improved through strengthened bonds with school. In order to feel connected, students must experience high expectations for academic success, feel supported by staff, and feel safe in their school. Increased school connectedness is related to educational motivation, classroom engagement, and better attendance. These are then linked to higher academic achievement. School connectedness is also related to lower rates of disruptive behavior, substance and tobacco use, emotional distress, and early age of first sex. School connectedness can be built through fair and consistent discipline, trust among all members of the school community, high expectations from the parents and school staff, effective

curriculum and teaching strategies, and students feeling connected to at least one member of the school staff. (p. 4)

Some may think of school connection in terms of participation in extracurricular activities (e.g., athletics, band, drama). However, school connection is much more than that. The majority of researchers currently studying school connection have included assessment of the student-adult relationship, along with students' perceptions of how valued and respected they feel at school and how connected they feel to their school.

To gauge students' feelings of school connection, we asked students in the Youth Voice Project to respond to three statements by choosing from five options: YES!, Yes, Unsure, No, and NO!

- I feel like I am part of this school.
- I feel valued and respected at school.
- I feel close to adults at my school.

To make comparisons, we coded each answer option with a number so that NO! = 1, No = 2, Unsure = 3, Yes = 4, and YES! = 5.

GENDER AND GRADE LEVEL EFFECTS

Past work has documented gender effects in favor of females (Crosnoe, Kirkpatrick, Johnson, & Elder, 2004; Pollack, 2004) and decline in school connection across grade level (Benson, Scales, Leffert, & Roehlkepartain, 1999; Eccles, Winfield, & Schiefele, 1998; Johnson, Crosnoe, & Elder, 2001; Moody & White, 2003). We therefore expected that females and students in earlier grades would report feeling closer to the adults at their school than would males and older students.

We wondered what happens to students' connections to school as they get older. For this question, our findings were consistent with past research. We found that students' *feelings of being part of their school* declined as they got older. Overall, females reported feeling more a part of their school than did males. Table 3.1 indicates these results.

There were no gender or grade level differences for feeling valued and respected in school. In other words, *feeling valued and respected at school* did not depend on students' grade level (see Table 3.2).

Feeling close to adults at school was different for males and females and varied by grade level. As expected, females reported feeling closer to adults at school than

Table 3.1: Gender and grade level effects for "I feel like I am part of this school"

	Males	Females
Elementary school	3.83	3.92
Middle school	3.76	3.88
High school	3.55	3.65

Table 3.2: Gender and grade level effects for "I feel valued and respected at school"

	Males	Females
Elementary school	3.30	3.21
Middle school	3.23	3.24
High school	3.23	3.17

males. In terms of grade level effects, students felt the closest to adults at school in elementary school, followed by middle school and high school (see Table 3.3). In elementary and middle school, we found that females felt closer to adults at school than did males. However, for high school students, no gender differences were found.

It is important to highlight that the overall scores for feeling close to an adult at school and for feeling valued and respected at school were relatively low for all students—that is, below 4 (4 represents an average answer of "Yes" but not "YES" in response to the question). These data suggest that, as educators, we need to do a better job promoting closer adult-student connections and respect for all students at school. The grade level effect suggests that we also need to find innovative strategies to better connect high school students to their schools, including improving connections between high school students and adults at school.

The gender effect suggests that males are significantly less likely to feel a part of their schools, when compared to females. Thus, it seems important to provide males with meaningful opportunities to connect to their schools in all grade levels.

It is also important to note that considerable variance from school to school existed in students' reports of connections to adults. In chapter 8, "A Tale of Two Schools," we will take a closer look at the highest and lowest performing schools with respect to school connection and adult responsiveness.

RELATIONSHIP BETWEEN SCHOOL CONNECTION AND TRAUMA LEVELS

After we looked at gender and grade level effects related to school connection variables, we wondered how students' associated trauma levels interact, if at all, with their school connection variables. To look at this question carefully, we conducted an analysis of variance to determine the effects of gender, grade level, and trauma level on school connection variables. Because this area of trauma and peer mis-

Table 3.3: Gender and grade level effects for "I feel close to adults at my school"

	Males	Females
Elementary school	3.34	3.72
Middle school	3.19	3.31
High school	3.00	3.13

treatment is relatively unexplored, we conducted a separate analysis for each connection variable to learn as much as we could. The following discussion describes the relationship between students' associated trauma levels and their school connection variables, while considering their grade level and gender.

I feel like I am part of this school

At all three grade levels and for both males and females, results showed that students experiencing mild trauma associated with their peer mistreatment reported feeling more part of their school (M = 3.96) than did students experiencing moderate to very severe trauma (M = 3.60). (See Table 3.4.)

I feel valued and respected at school

Similarly, results showed that students who reported mild trauma associated with peer mistreatment felt significantly more valued and respected at school (M = 3.54) than did their peers who reported moderate to very high trauma levels (M = 3.00). Again, this finding was true for students in all three grade levels and for both males and females (see Table 3.5).

I feel close to adults at my school

Unlike the other two school connection variables, the relationship between students' trauma levels associated with their peer mistreatment and feeling close to adults at school differed depending upon students' grade level. For example, in elementary and middle school, students' trauma levels were not related to how close they felt to adults at school. On the other hand, for high school students, those who experienced mild trauma related to their peer mistreatment felt closer to adults at school than did those students who experienced moderate to very severe trauma (see Table 3.6). This finding was true for both males and females.

An important point to make here is that high school students experiencing moderate to very severe trauma as a result of their peer mistreatment reported, on average, that they did not feel close to adults at school. This finding suggests that we may want to direct our prevention and intervention efforts toward those high school students who are repeatedly mistreated by their peers and who report moderate to very severe trauma. These high school students in particular may benefit from intentional positive connections with adults at school. These adult connec-

Table 3.4: Connection between trauma level and responses to "I feel like I am part of this school" separated by grade level

	Mild trauma (N=1,351)	Moderate to very severe trauma (N=1,578)
Elementary school	4.03	3.73
Middle school	3.96	3.66
High school	3.79	3.29

Note: 1=NO!, 3=Unsure, 5=YES!

Table 3.5: Connection between trauma level and responses to "I feel valued and respected at school" separated by grade level

	Mild trauma (N=1,351)	Moderate to very severe trauma (N=1,578)
Elementary school	3.64	3.06
Middle school	3.47	3.00
High school	3.46	2.83

Note: 1=NO!, 3=Unsure, 5=YES!

tions may take place through both overt formal mentoring programs and through informal efforts to build positive staff-student interaction.

CAN SCHOOL CONNECTION VARIABLES PROTECT AGAINST AND MITIGATE NEGATIVE EFFECTS OF PEER MISTREATMENT?

We know that not all children and youth experience the same effects from mistreatment by their peers. Consistent with this thinking, our data show that not all of the students who were repeatedly mistreated (i.e., at least two or three times a month) experienced moderate to very severe trauma. In fact, some of those students experienced only mild trauma associated with their peer mistreatment. As past research shows, how children respond to stressors depends on a range of factors, including individual characteristics (e.g., gender and age), the nature of the stressor itself (e.g., content and frequency of mistreatment), and contextual factors such as school related variables (Compas, Connor-Smith, Saltzman, Thomsen, & Wadsworth, 2001; Compas, Malcarne, & Fondacaro, 1988, Griffith, Dubow, & Ippolito, 2000).

The next survey question examined whether specific school connection variables (i.e., feel part of school, feel valued and respected at school, feel close to adults at school) influenced students' degree of trauma resulting from their peer mistreatment, while controlling for or taking into account students' gender and frequency of relational and physical victimization. In other words, do school connection variables significantly influence students' trauma levels over and above their gender and specific victimization experiences (including both relational and physical peer mistreatment)? This question is important to ask for a number of reasons. First, no

Table 3.6: Connection between trauma level and responses to "I feel close to adults at my school" separated by grade level

	Mild trauma (N=1,351)	Moderate to very severe trauma (N=1,578)
Elementary school	3.66	3.39
Middle school	3.27	3.23
High school	3.18	2.89

Note: 1=NO!, 3=Unsure, 5=YES!

matter what we do, there will always be some mistreatment of youth by their peers, thus making it imperative to identify possible protective factors that might reduce students' accompanying trauma levels. Second, if we can identify specific individual and contextual factors (i.e., specific school connection variables) that protect children and youth from experiencing more extreme forms of trauma associated with peer mistreatment, then we can use that information to inform subsequent prevention and intervention efforts.

To answer the question about the influence of school connection variables, we conducted a series of hierarchical linear regression models. Students' trauma levels associated with their peer mistreatment served as the dependent variable. Student response options were on a 4-point scale (mild, moderate, severe, and very severe). Students' gender (females were coded as 0 and males were coded as 1) was entered in the first step of the model. The second step included students' frequency of relational victimization and physical victimization. Scores ranged from 1 (never) to 5 (daily) for each form of victimization. The third step examined the relative contribution of all three school connection variables, above and beyond students' reports of victimization experiences and their gender. Interaction terms between each school connection variable (i.e., feel close to adults at school, feel part of school, and feel valued and respected at school) and gender were included in the fourth step. To control for developmental effects, we conducted a separate regression model for each grade level (i.e., elementary, middle, and high school).

Elementary school

In elementary school, school connection variables did not significantly affect students' reports of trauma above and beyond students' gender and frequency of peer mistreatment.

Middle school

In middle school, however, two of the three school connection variables did explain a difference in trauma levels when we controlled for gender and frequency of mistreatment. Students who reported that they felt part of their school and valued and respected at school reported lower trauma levels than those who did not. Interestingly, middle school students' reports of feeling close to adults at school did not affect their trauma levels.

High school

Mirroring the pattern for middle school students, high school students' reports of feeling part of school and feeling valued and respected at school were correlated with lower trauma levels. As with middle school students, feeling close to adults at school did not explain any unique variance in high school students' trauma levels.

These results suggest that school connection variables may play an important role in reducing students' perceived trauma levels associated with peer mistreatment.

We found that some school connection variables may be more important than others in terms of mitigating trauma levels related to peer mistreatment. Feeling part of school and feeling valued and respected at school influenced middle and high school students' trauma levels in a positive direction, whereas feeling close to adults at school did not affect students' trauma levels. Feeling part of school and feeling valued and respected at school was just as likely to serve as a positive buffer for girls as it was for boys.

Though we did not explore the responses of youth who mistreat others in the Youth Voice Project, other research has found that youth who mistreat others also report lower than average levels of connection to school. In an as-yet unpublished study surveying more than 1,600 youth in grades 5 through 8 from the southeastern part of the United States, Charisse and her colleagues examined the connection to school ("I feel close to people at this school") of youth who mistreated their peers at least two or three times a month and youth who were mistreated by their peers at least two or three times a month. For both relational and physical aggression, the less connected youth felt to school, the more likely they were to mistreat their peers. Whereas both youth who were mistreated and youth who mistreated others were significantly less connected to school, youth who mistreated others were even more disconnected from school than youth who were mistreated. The bottom line is that it is important to connect all students to school in meaningful ways.

STRATEGIES TO BUILD STUDENTS' SENSE OF CONNECTION TO SCHOOL

To quote Theodore Roosevelt, "People don't care how much you know until they know how much you care." When we take the time to communicate care and respect to our students on a daily basis, they subsequently become more open and responsive to learning, as well as to developing and maintaining relationships with us. We cannot underestimate students' needs to be valued and respected, particularly during adolescence.

As we have each talked with thousands of teachers and students nationwide, we have been reminded of some of the simple, yet significant, strategies we can use to communicate respect and value to our students and to build relationships. We have included some key items, though this is by no means an exhaustive list. We encourage you to think about the ways that you have successfully helped students feel that they belong and are valued and respected.

Greeting and welcoming youth

As we have each worked with schools in widespread locations, we have heard many anecdotes about the power of adults' taking the time to welcome young people to school. We hear about tough high schools that have been "turned around" when a new principal began standing by the front door and saying good morning to each student every day. We see teachers who take the time to say hello to or shake hands with every student on the way into the classroom. Implementing this intervention does not require extra money or training.

Carol Lieber (2002) describes a few commonsense strategies for greeting youth:

- Shake hands and say students' names as they walk in the door.

- As students arrive, make comments that let them know that you notice who they are.

- Say something about their appearance—a new hairstyle, a cool T-shirt, unusual earrings, a different color fingernail polish, a jacket you like, etc.

- Ask or comment about things that kids are doing outside of your classroom—sports events, extracurricular activities, and other events and projects that students participate in inside and outside of school.

- Give students specific positive feedback about something they've done well in class recently.

Young people who feel welcomed to school feel safer and are better able to learn. One research study, carried out with college students, makes the academic impact of these simple interactions clear. The study found that students in introductory psychology who were greeted personally by the teacher before class began did significantly better on a test that day than students who did not receive such attention (Weinstein, Laverghetta, Alexander, & Stewart, 2009). Another study demonstrated that teacher greetings increased the on-task behavior of middle school students who had been experiencing problems (Allday & Pakurar, 2007).

Perhaps the best authorities to cite are students themselves. At James Bean Elementary School in Maine, outgoing fifth-grade students were asked to write letters to school staff describing one positive thing staff did for them during the students' time at the school and the effects that action had. Every year, the most cited actions had to do with greeting, welcoming, and maintaining a positive feeling tone. The following are a few sample responses from these letters:

"When you say hello to me in the hall, I know I will have a great day."

"Last year my parents were fighting a lot and sometimes I was feeling really bad when I got on the bus. Every day Mr. Routhier [bus driver] said 'have a good day,' and I knew I would."

"Your smiles in the hallway always cheer me up."

As is apparent, it is not just teachers who contribute to students' sense of connection to school. Nonclassroom teachers and support staff also play an important role.

Listening to, getting to know, and sharing oneself with students

School staff can help students feel connected to school and build relationships with peers and staff when they listen to and try to get to know students. Some strategies to do this include listening to students' concerns (see chapter 6 for a closer look at effective listening) and structuring class activities to enhance opportunities for staff to really get to know students. Some strategies to encourage students to share their thoughts are "notes of concern" boxes, morning meetings, and daily check-ins.

Stan worked at Williams Junior High School in Oakland, Maine, in the early 2000s. At the time, the school held periodic "activity mornings." Staff members—including teachers, support staff, and the superintendent—identified an activity they would like to share with a small group of students for 2 hours. Students were given a list of activities, which did not include the name of the adult leader, and were asked to identify their first, second, and third choices. The organizers matched students to activities so that groups were reasonably even in size. This program allowed staff and students who shared interests a chance to spend time together doing something mutually enjoyable. Students formed connections with adults and peers with whom they might not otherwise have interacted. Participants found that the "glow" generated by each activity program lasted for some time.

We can build connections and inspire students when we share parts of our own lives with them. Students benefit from seeing adults struggle with their own learning process, whether that involves learning a new instrument, sport, or card game; mastering a new mathematical concept; or restoring a broken friendship. Too often, youth think that they are the only ones who find learning or friendships difficult, while in fact the majority of adults do as well. We have found that educators who continue to challenge themselves as lifelong learners can connect with young people by talking with them about their own learning process. We can model persistence in the face of frustration and disappointment, and we can help youth remain focused on their goals despite challenging obstacles. Students are more likely to become passionate learners when they see adults they respect voluntarily focusing time and energy on learning. Our students also benefit when they hear about why we have chosen to teach a particular subject or enter a particular field of study.

Though we encourage adults to share parts of their lives with their students, we caution adults to limit some types of sharing. Sometimes adults are tempted to edit their life stories to present an unrealistically positive model to students. There is certainly some value in such editing because youth are unlikely to benefit from hearing about serious relationship problems or our struggles with depression or self-destructive behavior. On the other hand, young people do benefit from hearing about our struggles. We should share those stories that students will benefit from hearing.

A collaborative approach

Research conducted by Janis Whitlock (2006) gives us a clue as to how we might enhance students' feelings of school connection. Whitlock found that school connectedness is enhanced when students have the opportunity to have meaningful input into school policies and are actively engaged by class material. Both of these factors are consistent with schools' adopting a collaborative approach that values student voices within the classroom as well as within the structure of the school environment. In chapter 8, we describe one school's collaborative approach to developing and reinforcing a districtwide code of ethics.

The value of the collaborative approach is highlighted in the Caring School Community, a program adapted from the Child Development Project, designed for elementary age students (Battistich, Solomon, Watson, & Schaps, 1997; Battistich, Watson, Solomon, Schaps, & Solomon, 1991a, 1991b, 1991c). This whole-school approach is a multi-year initiative that promotes caring communities of learners through meaningful, active collaboration between and among students, staff, and parents. The program consists of four elements: class meeting lessons, cross-age buddies, homeside activities, and schoolwide community building. Class meeting lessons provide teachers and students with a forum to get to know one another, discuss issues, identify and solve problems collaboratively, and make a range of decisions that affect classroom life. Cross-age buddies involves pairing whole classes of older and younger students for academic and recreational activities that build caring cross-age relationships and create a schoolwide climate of trust. Homeside activities are short conversational activities that are sent home with students for them to do with their parents or caregivers and then to discuss in their classrooms. Schoolwide community building brings students, parents, and school staff together to create new school traditions.

CHAPTER 4

Self-Actions

Life is 10% of what happens to us and 90% of how we respond.

—*John Maxwell, evangelical pastor and author*

As adults who work with young people, we've often found ourselves giving advice to mistreated youth. Yet we realized that we didn't know if our advice was actually helping or hurting. In the Youth Voice Project, we wanted to tap into the expertise of young people. Clearly, they are growing up in a world adults will never fully understand. We need to listen to their experiences before telling them what we think they should do.

Typically, mistreated youth have been told to stick up for themselves, be less reactive and show less emotion, hit or retaliate, or forget about it. Often both youth and adults working in this field hear contradictory advice. When designing the survey, we gathered input from youth and adults to come up with a list of possible self-actions youth could use in response to peer mistreatment. In the survey itself, we gave young people four options for each self-action:

- I didn't do this.
- I did it and things got worse.
- I did it and nothing changed.
- I did it and things got better.

We also asked youth to write about what they did in their own words. This approach allowed us to collect both quantitative and qualitative data.

To compare and contrast actions, we created an average helpfulness score for each self-action. We coded "things got better" as 1, "nothing changed" as 0, and "things got worse" as negative 1, then averaged results for each action. We also wanted to learn as much as we could about each action. For example, we wanted to find out if specific self-actions were more helpful for girls than for boys and vice versa. We wanted to find out if elementary school students found different self-actions helpful, as compared with middle school or high school students. These are important questions to ask as we begin to think about effective intervention programs.

TYPES OF SELF-ACTIONS

We categorized the twelve self-actions into the following eight categories.

Using humor

Made a joke about it.

Accessing support

Told an adult at home.

Told a friend.

Told an adult at school.

Reframing the situation

Reminded myself that what they are doing is not my fault and that THEY are the ones who are doing something wrong.

Avoidance

Pretended it didn't bother me.

Walked away.

Did nothing

Did nothing.

Revenge

Made plans to get back at them or fight them.

Hit them or fought them.

I-messages

Told the person or people how I felt about what they were doing.

Direct confrontation

Told the person or people to stop.

WHAT ARE THE MOST HELPFUL SELF-ACTIONS?

Overall, we found that the most helpful self-actions students used in response to peer mistreatment fell into the categories of using humor, accessing support, and reframing the situation (see Table 4.1). The least helpful actions fell into the categories of direct confrontation, I-messages, did nothing, and revenge. We found significant differences in the helpfulness of actions based on students' gender and grade level.

Throughout the book, we will use boldface type to indicate the actions that youth told us were likely to make things better, regular type to indicate the actions that were about as likely to make things worse as they were to make things better, and italic type to indicate the actions likely to make things worse.

Elementary school

Elementary school boys reported humor and accessing support as the only helpful self-actions, whereas elementary school girls were helped only by accessing support. Although reframing the situation was a helpful action overall, it was not particularly

Table 4.1: Overall helpfulness of students' self-actions (N=2,929)

	Helpfulness score
Made a joke about it	.28
Told a friend	.21
Told an adult at home	.21
Reminded myself that what they are doing is not my fault and that THEY are the ones who are doing something wrong	.17
Told an adult at school	.12
Walked away	.06
Pretended it didn't bother me	.05
Hit them or fought them	.00
Did nothing	−.05
Made plans to get back at them or fight them	−.05
Told the person or people how I felt about what they were doing	−.07
Told the person or people to stop	−.09

helpful for elementary school students. Of all three groups of grade levels, elementary school students reported the worst outcomes from the least helpful actions in the categories of avoidance, did nothing, and revenge (see Tables 4.2 and 4.3).

Middle school

Results show that as students got older, they became more effective at using a wider range of actions. Using humor, accessing support, reframing the situation, and

Table 4.2: Helpfulness of self-actions for elementary school males (N=150)

	Helpfulness score
Made a joke about it	.30
Told an adult at home	.27
Told an adult at school	.23
Told a friend	.22
Walked away	.06
Reminded myself that what they are doing is not my fault and that THEY are the ones who are doing something wrong	.06
Pretended it didn't bother me	−.04
Told the person or people how I felt about what they were doing	−.12
Told the person or people to stop	−.15
Did nothing	−.21
Made plans to get back at them or fight them	−.60
Hit them or fought them	−.74

Table 4.3: Helpfulness of self-actions for elementary school females (N=168)

	Helpfulness score
Told an adult at school	.33
Told an adult at home	.26
Told a friend	.15
Reminded myself that what they are doing is not my fault and that THEY are the ones who are doing something wrong	−.01
Told the person or people how I felt about what they were doing	−.01
Walked away	−.04
Made a joke about it	−.13
Told the person or people to stop	−.16
Pretended it didn't bother me	−.17
Hit them or fought them	−.20
Did nothing	−.21
Made plans to get back at them or fight them	−.60

avoidance were all helpful actions for middle school males (see Table 4.4). Middle school females reported similar results—they found using humor, accessing support, and reframing the situation helpful (see Table 4.5). The most harmful self-actions for middle school males were direct confrontation and I-messages, whereas the most harmful actions for females were avoidance and revenge.

Table 4.4: Helpfulness of self-actions for middle school males (N=809)

	Helpfulness score
Made a joke about it	.32
Told an adult at home	.19
Told a friend	.17
Reminded myself that what they are doing is not my fault and that THEY are the ones who are doing something wrong	.17
Told an adult at school	.15
Walked away	.11
Pretended it didn't bother me	.09
Did nothing	.04
Hit them or fought them	−.07
Made plans to get back at them or fight them	−.09
Told the person or people to stop	−.12
Told the person or people how I felt about what they were doing	−.14

Table 4.5: Helpfulness of self-actions for middle school females (N=806)

	Helpfulness score
Made a joke about it	.30
Told a friend	.23
Told an adult at home	.23
Reminded myself that what they are doing is not my fault and that THEY are the ones who are doing something wrong	.20
Told an adult at school	.12
Pretended it didn't bother me	.00
Walked away	−.01
Told the person or people how I felt about what they were doing	−.06
Hit them or fought them	−.06
Told the person or people to stop	−.06
Did nothing	−.10
Made plans to get back at them or fight them	−.16

High school

High school students reported a wider range of helpful self-actions, including using humor, revenge, accessing support, reframing the situation, and avoidance for males (see Table 4.6) and using humor, reframing the situation, and accessing support for females (see Table 4.7). High school males reported that the least helpful

Table 4.6: Helpfulness of self-actions for high school males (N=429)

	Helpfulness score
Made a joke about it	.32
Hit them or fought them	.29
Told a friend	.23
Made plans to get back at them or fight them	.22
Reminded myself that what they are doing is not my fault and that THEY are the ones who are doing something wrong	.20
Walked away	.17
Pretended it didn't bother me	.16
Told an adult at home	.14
Told the person or people to stop	.02
Did nothing	.02
Told an adult at school	−.07
Told the person or people how I felt about what they were doing	−.10

Table 4.7: Helpfulness of self-actions for high school females (N=444)

	Helpfulness score
Made a joke about it	.26
Reminded myself that what they are doing is not my fault and that THEY are the ones who are doing something wrong	.24
Told a friend	.24
Told an adult at home	.22
Walked away	.10
Pretended it didn't bother me	.09
Told the person or people how I felt about what they were doing	.04
Told an adult at school	–.01
Told the person or people to stop	–.01
Did nothing	–.07
Made plans to get back at them or fight them	–.07
Hit them or fought them	–.13

actions were accessing support by telling an adult at school and using I-messages. High school females reported that revenge was the least helpful action.

Results from high school males give us particular cause for concern. Though revenge was often described as making things better for high school males, this does not mean that we should advise them to engage in these actions. How do we ever really know when the score is even? When is it enough? The risks of aggression for the aggressor and target are clear. In discouraging violence as a method of resolving difficulties, we are guided by Gandhi, who wrote, "I object to violence because when it appears to do good, the good is only temporary; the evil it does is permanent." We need to make sure that high school boys have positive and effective alternatives to revenge.

High school students were the only group to report that telling adults at school about peer mistreatment led to negative outcomes about as often as it led to positive outcomes. In chapter 6, we will explore what adults at school are saying to high school students that might discourage them from reporting mistreatment. Telling or asking mistreating peers to stop rarely worked for any mistreated youth.

We need to understand that when we ask youth to solve problems of mistreatment themselves without providing the necessary supports and skills, we may be pushing them toward establishing and maintaining aggressive behavior. As a wise third-grade teacher once told Charisse, youth need skills and support to solve problems. Without those skills and supports, only the strong get stronger. To reduce the frequency of aggressive behavior patterns, we must change adult and peer behavior so that mistreated youth have effective, alternate pathways to positive outcomes. Giving high school boys, in particular, better ways to solve their problems can make schools safer for all students.

USING HUMOR

As shown in Table 4.8, the category of using humor in response to peer mistreatment included one self-action: made a joke about it. Overall, this action was the most helpful self-action in response to peer mistreatment. The effectiveness of using humor varied by gender and grade level. This action also was significantly more helpful for males than it was for females. This gender effect does not surprise us, given the current culture that encourages boys to tease and repress negative feelings (except anger), especially those negative feelings involving vulnerability (Pollack, 2004).

Middle and high school students reported more success using humor than did younger children. This developmental effect is consistent with research documenting children's increased social and cognitive skills over time (Selman, 1980). Moreover, middle and high school students are inclined to try on new roles and seek attention while simultaneously trying to fit in. Using humor may be a relatively safe approach to meeting these developmental challenges.

It is important to note that we don't know how or exactly why humor was helpful. We reviewed students' text responses and discovered that young people who used this strategy rarely wrote that their use of humor stopped the mistreatment. Instead, many of them wrote about how they felt better after using humor. Often the humor was internal or used in a healing way with friends after the incident. One student wrote, "When I said I know I'm short and laughed with their jokes, they didn't stop, but it was easier to handle."

Klein and Kuiper (2006) describe different types of humor that youth can use in response to bullying. They describe *adaptive humor* as including affiliative humor, which enhances one's relationships, and self-enhancing humor, a beneficial coping strategy that helps the person maintain a positive outlook on life. In contrast, they describe *aggressive humor*, which uses sarcasm to attack others, and *self-defeating humor*,

Table 4.8: Gender and grade level effects for "made a joke about it"

	Helpfulness score
All mistreated students	.28
Males	.32
Females	.26
Elementary school	.08
Middle school	.30
High school	.29

which is self-disparaging. Klein and Kuiper state that youth who employ aggressive or self-defeating forms of humor may place themselves at greater risk of being victimized.

In reviewing the text responses of youth who reported that they made a joke about what happened and that things then got better, we found examples of affiliative humor (joked about it with my friends) and self-enhancing humor (thought a joke about it). We found no examples of aggressive (sarcastic) or self-defeating (self-disparaging) humor in these students' accounts of what actually helped them. This finding is in marked contrast to some popular advice about using humor in bullying situations, in which self-disparaging humor is often advised. Klein and Kuiper (2006) state:

> Those using self-enhancing humor have a humorous outlook on life and can maintain a humorous perspective, even when faced with potentially stressful events and situations. These individuals also use humor as a beneficial coping strategy to minimize negative emotions, while still maintaining a realistic perspective on life. Self-enhancing humor thus serves to buffer and protect the self, but not at the expense of others.

Affiliative humor focuses on the use of humor to enhance interpersonal and social relationships. Humor is employed here to raise group morale, identity, and cohesiveness by reducing conflicts and increasing others' feelings of well being. This nonhostile use of humor also involves joking and banter to reduce interpersonal tensions and facilitate relationships with others.

In contrast to the two adaptive styles, which are tolerant and accepting of both self and others, the two maladaptive styles are detrimental and potentially injurious to either the self (i.e., self-defeating humor) or others (i.e., aggressive humor). Those who employ self-defeating humor, for example, use excessive self-disparaging and ingratiating humor in inappropriate attempts to gain the approval of others and thus enhance their interpersonal relationships. Humor is expressed in a self-detrimental style that is at high personal cost. Rod Martin and his colleagues at the University of Western Ontario have studied how individual differences in the use of humor relate to psychological well-being (Martin, Puhlik-Doris, Larsen, Gray, & Weir, 2003). Their findings suggest that individuals displaying high levels of self-defeating humor may use this style to hide underlying negative feelings or to avoid dealing constructively with a problem. These individuals are characterized by elements of avoidance, emotional neediness, and low self-esteem.

The final maladaptive style is described as aggressive humor. Here, individuals may use a variety of negative humor techniques (including teasing, ridicule, sarcasm, and disparagement) to denigrate and put down others. Aggressive humor is displayed with little regard for its potential negative impact on others, including ultimately alienating these individuals and seriously impairing social and interpersonal relationships (Martin et al., 2003).

These different types of humor require further exploration. In a future version of the questionnaire, we plan to distinguish between these types of humor to learn how students use humor to cope with peer mistreatment.

ACCESSING SUPPORT

The category of accessing support included three self-actions: "told an adult at school," "told a friend," and "told an adult at home." We found that no matter their grade level or gender, when mistreated students told a friend or an adult at home about their mistreatment, things were likely to get better.

Telling a friend and telling an adult at home about peer mistreatment were somewhat more helpful than telling an adult at school. Telling an adult at school was less helpful for older students than it was for younger students. In fact, telling an adult at school about what happened was among the most helpful self-actions for younger students, whereas for high school students this action was about as likely to make things worse as to make them better (see Table 4.9). We found no gender differences.

Table 4.9: Grade level effects for "told an adult at school"

	Helpfulness score
All mistreated students	.12
Elementary school	.25
Middle school	.14
High school	−.05

This grade level effect is consistent with research showing the growing importance of peer relationships during the adolescent years (Brown, 2004; Cobb, 2010; Steinberg & Silverberg, 1986). By high school, students spend more time with their friends than with their own family (Larson, Richards, Moneta, Holmbeck, & Duckett, 1996), and peers become their primary support system (Furman & Buhrmester, 1992; Levitt, Guacci, Franco, & Levitt, 1993). With that said, we know that high school students still benefit from connections with adults. These results should urge those of us who work with high school students to increase our efforts to connect with them and take meaningful action to help them when they tell us about peer mistreatment.

To explore the question of adult influence further, we looked at students' reports of how *close* they felt to adults at school. We found that the helpfulness of telling an adult at school seemed to parallel students' reports of closeness to adults at their schools (see Table 4.10). In other words, those students who felt closer to an adult at school were more likely to tell an adult at school about their experiences related to peer mistreatment. It could be, then, that "feeling close to an adult at school" is an important variable in reducing students' trauma levels related to their peer mistreatment.

Is it possible that feeling close to an adult at school actually mediates the relationship between students' peer mistreatment and their associated trauma levels? To look at this question, we conducted Sobel's mediation test. As shown in Figure 4.1, a mediating variable can change the impact of X on Y—in this case feeling close to an adult at school may alter the impact of peer mistreatment on students' accompanying trauma levels. Said simply, we wanted to know if feeling close to an adult at school drove

Table 4.10: A comparison of the helpfulness of "told an adult at school" with feelings of closeness to adults at school

	Helpfulness score for "told an adult at school"	Average score for "I feel close to adults at my school" (1=NO!, 3=Unsure, 5=YES!)
All mistreated students	.12	3.21
Elementary school	.25	3.45
Middle school	.14	3.25
High school	−.05	3.05

the relationship between students' peer mistreatment (including both relational and physical peer mistreatment) and their reported trauma levels. Knowing that females report more trauma than males, we controlled for gender in the analysis. Because of the developmental trends described previously (e.g., younger children are more likely to report feeling close to an adult at school), we conducted three separate mediation tests for each grade level—elementary school students, middle school students, and high school students.

Our results were surprising. Although elementary students on average reported feeling closer to adults at school, that adult relationship did not mediate the connection between their peer mistreatment and associated trauma levels ($p = .23$). Similarly, among middle school students, feeling close to adults at school did not mediate their relationship between peer mistreatment and trauma levels ($p = .81$). However, feeling close to adults at school *did* mediate the connection between peer mistreatment and students' associated trauma levels among high school students ($p = .04$). In other words, when accounting for relational and physical mistreatment and controlling for any gender effects, high school students who felt closer to adults at school reported less trauma associated with their peer mistreatment. It therefore seems that feeling close to an adult at school is a very important variable, particularly among high school students. In sum, in terms of positively influencing trauma levels related to peer mistreatment, at the high school level it is less about telling an adult at school and more about the relationship between the high school student and the adult.

Figure 4.1: Mediation Model for "Feel Close"

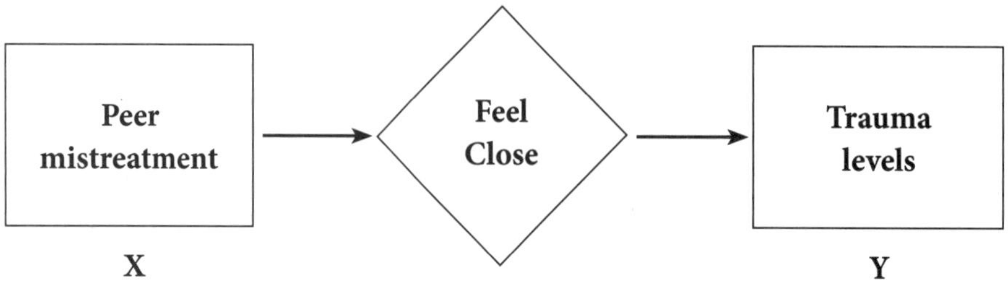

REFRAMING THE SITUATION

The category of reframing the situation included one self-action: "reminded myself that what they are doing is not my fault and that THEY are the ones who are doing something wrong." Results from our analysis showed that this type of reframing was much more helpful for older students than for younger students (see Table 4.11). This grade level effect is not surprising given the advanced cognitive skills and social sophistication needed to use this action effectively (Hudley & Graham, 1993; Crick, Grotpeter, & Bigbee, 2002). For younger students, the use of this self-action was just as likely to make things worse as it was to make things better. No gender differences were found.

Youth participating in the Youth Voice Project wrote about their successes and failures reframing others' negative words and actions in the following ways:

> "[I] just forgot about it and told myself that I have great friends who do respect me and didn't listen to what other people thought of me."

> "[I] just thought a joke about it."

What happens when students frame a situation negatively? As the following response shows, significant negative consequences can arise when students are unable to reframe the situation and instead allow negative statements to become part of their ongoing self-talk.

> "A girl said that I was ugly, and everyday I would cry, I wouldn't eat, I'd obsess over my weight—every 5 seconds I'd think about what others thought of me. To this day, I'm still hurt, emotionally scarred, and I continue to worry about my weight."

AVOIDANCE AND DID NOTHING

The category of avoidance included two self-actions in response to peer mistreatment: "pretended it didn't bother me" and "walked away." These two actions were relatively ineffective; only "did nothing" had a less positive impact.

Using avoidance strategies to address peer mistreatment was particularly harmful for elementary school students. Things generally got worse when elementary students did nothing or pretended it didn't bother them. Interestingly, a somewhat different

Table 4.11: Grade level effects for "reminded myself that what they are doing is not my fault and that THEY are the ones who are doing something wrong"

	Helpfulness score
All mistreated students	.17
Elementary school	.01
Middle school	.19
High school	.22

Table 4.12: Grade level effects for "did nothing"

	Helpfulness score
All mistreated students	−.05
Elementary school	−.23
Middle school	−.03
High school	−.02

trend emerged for high school students. That is, for mistreated high school students, walking away or pretending it didn't bother them were somewhat helpful. Among mistreated middle school students, "pretended it didn't bother me," "walked away," and "did nothing" were just as likely to make things worse as to make things better.

Though doing nothing was likely to make things worse in elementary school, it was just as likely to make things better as to make things worse in middle and high school. No gender effects were found (see Table 4.12). On average, pretending the mistreatment didn't bother them had around a 50–50 chance of leading to positive or negative outcomes. However, as shown in Table 4.13, this strategy was more likely to lead to negative outcomes for elementary students and more likely to lead to positive outcomes for high school students. No gender effects were found.

Overall, the helpfulness of walking away was similar to the helpfulness of "pretended it didn't bother me." Walking away was more helpful for older students than for younger students (Table 4.14). A gender effect also emerged, suggesting that walking away was more helpful for males than it was for females.

Why is walking away more helpful than doing nothing? Although it may be tempting to conceptualize these strategies as similar in nature, one could argue that when mistreated students walk away they are, in effect, doing something. In addition, in our experience, as youth get older they are more likely to have a group of peers to walk toward as they walk away from mistreatment.

Choosing to do nothing in response to a negative experience, on the other hand, can be dangerous business. As Martin Seligman, director of the Positive Psychology Center at the University of Pennsylvania, as well as others, have reminded

Table 4.13: Grade level effects for "pretended it didn't bother me"

	Helpfulness score
All mistreated students	.05
Elementary school	−.11
Middle school	.04
High school	.12

Table 4.14: Grade level and gender effects for "walked away"

	Helpfulness score
All mistreated students	.06
Elementary school	−.01
Middle school	.05
High school	.13
Males	.12
Females	.02

us (e.g., Peterson, Maier, & Seligman, 1993), doing nothing can result in "learned helplessness." Each time young people respond to a negative experience by doing nothing, they are reinforcing the notion that they are unable to take effective action. In essence, it is those behaviors we practice over and over again that become etched in our neural pathways and eventually become habit. Changing our response patterns is difficult at any age. However, for students with a long history of experiences this process may be particularly tough. Our job as caring adults and educators is to empower our youth to respond to negative experiences in constructive ways.

REVENGE

The revenge category included two self-actions: "made plans to get back at them or fight them" and "hit them or fought them." On average, both of these self-actions led to things getting worse about as often as they led to things getting better. Both actions were among the most harmful for elementary school students. Middle school students found them around as likely to make things better as to make things worse, and high school students, on average, reported these actions as slightly more helpful than unhelpful. Females experienced worse outcomes from using these actions (see Tables 4.15 and 4.16).

Table 4.15: Grade level and gender effects for "made plans to get back at them or fight them"

	Helpfulness score
All mistreated students	−.05
Elementary school	−.42
Middle school	−.10
High school	.12
Males	−.01
Females	−.16

Table 4.16: Grade level and gender effects for "hit them or fought them"

	Helpfulness score
All mistreated students	.00
Elementary school	−.46
Middle school	−.05
High school	.19
Males	.02
Females	−.09

I-MESSAGES

The I-messages category included one self-action: "told the person or people how I felt about what they were doing." Overall, using I-messages as a response to peer mistreatment was about as likely to make things better as to make them worse. This action was not helpful for females; however, it was significantly less helpful for males (see Table 4.17), and the helpfulness did not depend on students' grade level.

DIRECT CONFRONTATION

The category of direct confrontation consisted of one self-action: "told the person or people to stop." Overall, this was the least helpful self-action. For mistreated elementary and middle school students, this strategy tended to make things worse. Among high school students who used this action, things were about as likely to get worse as they were to get better (see Table 4.18). There were no gender effects.

PREVALENCE OF SELF-ACTIONS

Unfortunately, we found that many students are using actions that aren't helping them (see Table 4.19). Youth were most likely to use self-actions focused on avoidance, accessing support, direct confrontation, and reframing the situation. There were significant differences by grade level and gender. Overall, three of the four most commonly used actions were not particularly helpful.

These data suggest that youth are listening to adults. They have heard the following advice from adults for years: "Walk away," "Don't act like a victim," "Pretend it doesn't bother you," "Tell the person how you feel," and "Tell the person to stop." Much of this advice showed up in the form of the most prevalent self-actions. How-

Table 4.17: Gender effects for "told the person or people how I felt about what they were doing"

	Helpfulness score
All mistreated students	−.07
Males	−.13
Females	−.02

Table 4.18: Grade level and gender effects for "told the person or people to stop"

	Helpfulness score
All mistreated students	−.09
Elementary school	−.15
Middle school	−.13
High school	.00

ever, and this is crucial, youth reported that these actions were unlikely to lead to positive outcomes and, in fact, some tended to make things worse, especially for elementary school children. Overall, only one of the four most commonly used self-actions led to things getting better: Telling a friend.

On a positive note, we found support-seeking actions to be common and helpful. More than half of mistreated students sought support from friends, adults at home, and/or adults at school. Telling a friend was the most common and telling an adult at school was the least common support-seeking strategy. Older students were more likely to tell their friends about peer mistreatment than were younger students. Although this is expected in terms of the developmental nature of friendships, it might behoove us as caring adults to help younger children effectively share their negative peer experiences with a trusted friend.

Elementary school students

For elementary school students, self-actions were even less effective than for youth overall. The most common self-action among elementary school males was more

Table 4.19: Overall prevalence and helpfulness of self-actions (N=2,929)

	Prevalence rate	Helpfulness score
Pretended it didn't bother me	72%	.05
Told a friend	63%	.21
Told the person or people to stop	62%	−.09
Walked away	62%	.06
Reminded myself that what they are doing is not my fault and that THEY are the ones who are doing something wrong	55%	.17
Told an adult at home	45%	.21
Did nothing	43%	−.05
Made a joke about it	38%	.28
Told the person or people how I felt about what they were doing	35%	−.07
Told an adult at school	30%	.12
Made plans to get back at them or fight them	26%	−.05
Hit them or fought them	18%	.00

Table 4.20: Prevalence and helpfulness of self-actions for elementary school males (N=150)

	Prevalence rate	Helpfulness score
Told the person or people to stop	71%	−.15
Pretended it didn't bother me	66%	−.04
Walked away	61%	.06
Told an adult at home	59%	.27
Told a friend	58%	.22
Reminded myself that what they are doing is not my fault and that THEY are the ones who are doing something wrong	56%	.06
Told an adult at school	50%	.23
Told the person or people how I felt about what they were doing	44%	−.12
Did nothing	39%	−.21
Made plans to get back at them or fight them	20%	−.60
Made a joke about it	19%	.30
Hit them or fought them	13%	−.74

harmful than helpful, and only three of the seven actions elementary school males used at least half the time were likely to lead to positive outcomes (see Table 4.20). Similarly, the two most commonly used actions by elementary school females were harmful, and only three of the eight most commonly used actions were helpful (see Table 4.21).

Table 4.21: Prevalence and helpfulness of self-actions for elementary school females (N=168)

	Prevalence rate	Helpfulness score
Pretended it didn't bother me	66%	−.17
Told the person or people to stop	66%	−.17
Walked away	63%	−.04
Told an adult at home	62%	.26
Told a friend	61%	.15
Reminded myself that what they are doing is not my fault and that THEY are the ones who are doing something wrong	59%	−.01
Told the person or people how I felt about what they were doing	50%	−.01
Told an adult at school	50%	.33
Did nothing	34%	−.25
Made plans to get back at them or fight them	20%	−.39
Made a joke about it	19%	−.13
Hit them or fought them	6%	−.20

Among elementary school students, we found a significant relationship between gender and prevalence for just three self-actions. Males were more likely than females to hit or fight peers in response to being mistreated and to tell the person or people to stop. Females were more likely than males to tell the person or people how they felt about what they did.

Middle school students

A majority of middle school students also used ineffective self-actions. The most common self-actions for this age group fell into the categories of avoidance, accessing support, and direct confrontation. Of the actions used by at least half the mistreated students surveyed, three of five actions were helpful for males (see Table 4.22) and three of six were helpful for females (see Table 4.23).

We found that males and females in middle school were likely to use different actions. Females were more likely to tell an adult at home, tell a friend, pretend it didn't bother them, walk away, and tell the person or people how they felt about what they did. Males were more likely to make a joke about it, do nothing, make plans to get back at them or fight them, and hit them or fight them.

In general, females were more likely to respond to peer mistreatment with helpful actions, whereas males were more likely to use less helpful actions, with a few exceptions. These findings suggest that adults should help males access more helpful self-actions, such as support-seeking strategies. It may be valuable to train males how to talk to friends and adults at home about experiences related to peer mistreatment. Role-plays and meaningful activities that strengthen positive relationships between males and their friends as well as males and adults might make

Table 4.22: Prevalence and helpfulness of self-actions for middle school males (N=809)

	Prevalence rate	Helpfulness score
Pretended it didn't bother me	72%	.09
Told the person or people to stop	64%	−.12
Walked away	63%	.11
Told a friend	63%	.17
Reminded myself that what they are doing is not my fault and that THEY are the ones who are doing something wrong	53%	.17
Told an adult at home	47%	.19
Did nothing	42%	.04
Made a joke about it	35%	.32
Told the person or people how I felt about what they were doing	32%	−.14
Told an adult at school	30%	.15
Made plans to get back at them or fight them	24%	−.09
Hit them or fought them	18%	−.07

Table 4.23: Prevalence and helpfulness of self-actions for middle school females (N=806)

	Prevalence rate	Helpfulness score
Pretended it didn't bother me	75%	.00
Told a friend	72%	.23
Walked away	66%	−.01
Told the person or people to stop	64%	−.13
Reminded myself that what they are doing is not my fault and that THEY are the ones who are doing something wrong	55%	.20
Told an adult at home	53%	.23
Did nothing	40%	−.10
Told the person or people how I felt about what they were doing	36%	−.06
Made a joke about it	30%	.30
Told an adult at school	29%	.12
Made plans to get back at them or fight them	18%	−.16
Hit them or fought them	11%	−.06

it more likely that they will seek support. In addition, middle school males may need additional training around the negative outcomes of using revenge. Most important, when adults respond more effectively to students' reports of mistreatment, revenge becomes less necessary.

High school students

Out of all grade levels, high school students were most likely to use helpful self-actions, though this is partially due to the fact that high school students were more effective at using a wider variety of self-actions. The most common self-actions among high school students fell into the categories of avoidance, accessing support, direct confrontation, and reframing the situation. Of the actions used by at least half the mistreated high school students surveyed, five of six actions were helpful for males (see Table 4.24) and four of six actions were helpful for females (see Table 4.25).

High school students were less likely than elementary or middle school students to tell an adult, either at home or at school, about their peer mistreatment. This finding is consistent with a culture that promotes two very separate worlds—an adolescent world and an adult world. Though it is natural for teenagers to develop deeper relationships with their peers over time, we believe that cultural isolation robs our adolescents of the significant benefits of having meaningful relationships with adults at a time in their lives that is full of transition, uncertainty, and change.

As is the case for middle school students, males and females in high school often used different actions. Females were more likely to tell an adult at home, tell a friend, pretend it didn't bother them, remind themselves that it wasn't their fault,

Table 4.24: Prevalence and helpfulness of self-actions for high school males (N=429)

	Prevalence rate	Helpfulness score
Pretended it didn't bother me	73%	.16
Told a friend	65%	.23
Walked away	59%	.17
Told the person to stop	57%	.02
Reminded myself that what they are doing is not my fault and that THEY are the ones who are doing something wrong	57%	.20
Made a joke about it	53%	.32
Did nothing	46%	.02
Told the person or people how I felt about what they were doing	38%	–.10
Told an adult at home	37%	.14
Made plans to get back at them or fight them	31%	.22
Told an adult at school	22%	–.07
Hit them or fought them	21%	.29

and walk away. High school males were more likely to make a joke about it, make plans to get back at them or fight them, and hit them or fight them.

CONNECTION BETWEEN SELF-ACTIONS AND TRAUMA LEVELS

Mistreated students who experienced mild trauma were more likely to make a joke about the situation, but they were less likely than students who experienced

Table 4.25: Prevalence and helpfulness of self-actions for high school females (N=444)

	Prevalence rate	Helpfulness score
Pretended it didn't bother me	81%	.09
Told a friend	76%	.24
Walked away	66%	.10
Reminded myself that what they are doing is not my fault and that THEY are the ones who are doing something wrong	65%	.24
Told the person or people to stop	60%	–.01
Made a joke about it	51%	.26
Did nothing	48%	–.07
Told the person or people how I felt about what they were doing	38%	.04
Told an adult at home	41%	.22
Told an adult at school	23%	–.01
Made plans to get back at them or fight them	23%	–.07
Hit them or fought them	12%	–.13

moderate to very severe trauma to tell a friend and to tell an adult at home. Students who experienced mild trauma used the three most harmful actions less often: They were less likely to make plans to get back at them or fight them, tell the person or people how they felt about what they were doing, and tell the person or people to stop (see Table 4.26).

ENCOURAGING HELPFUL SELF-ACTIONS

In helping mistreated youth develop and implement helpful self-actions, we should be careful not to place responsibility for healing solely on those students. It is not the responsibility of mistreated youth to "get over it." However, together with a strong foundation of disciplinary, restorative interventions—and supportive adult and peer actions—we can encourage all youth to develop resiliency and effective methods to solve problems and handle adversity.

Self-efficacy

One of our primary goals in these efforts is to help youth develop self-efficacy. *Self-efficacy,* a term first defined by Albert Bandura (1977), is the belief in our own capabilities to be successful. Bandura (1994) has demonstrated the value of encouraging children to believe they have the skills needed to stand strong in the face of peer mistreatment. In order to build self-efficacy, adults can verbally encourage youth and provide opportunities for youth to practice helpful responses to peer mistreatment. This can strengthen students' sense of self-efficacy and, subsequently, their resiliency.

One of the primary ways adults can promote self-efficacy is by not suggesting self-actions that are unlikely to work. As we've said, many of the self-actions youth use most often are relatively ineffective but often recommended by adults. Before giving advice, adults should listen and ask open-ended questions about

Table 4.26: Prevalence and helpfulness scores for the most and least helpful self-actions separated by trauma level

	Helpfulness score	Mild trauma (N=1,351)	Moderate to very severe trauma (N=1,578)
Made a joke about it	.28	47%	31%
Told a friend(s)	.21	59%	66%
Told an adult at home	.21	34%	55%
Made plans to get back at them or fight them	–.05	24%	28%
Told the person or people how I felt about what they were doing	–.07	28%	41%
Told the person or people to stop	–.09	56%	68%

YOUTH VOICES: SELF-ACTIONS

We asked students three open-ended questions about self-actions.

- Overall, what did you do that helped the most?
- What happened when you did that?
- What else do you wish you had done?

The following responses are from students who reported mild trauma associated with peer mistreatment.

Native Hawaiian female in fifth grade

Overall, what did you do that helped you the most?

i told my friends and they agreed with me which made me feel better, and told my mom so someone that could actually help knew, but i told my mom not to help unless it got worse.

What happened when you did that?

it gave me a better outlook on the situation.

What else do you wish you had done?

i think i am handling it well because the situation is not worsening.

Male in seventh grade, unknown race

Overall, what did you do that helped you the most?

making a joke about the whole incident.

What happened when you did that?

i felt better.

African American female in eighth grade

Overall, what did you do that helped you the most?

Tell parents it relieved it off my chest.

What happened when you did that?

I felt a lot better.

White female in eighth grade

Over all, what did you do that helped you the most?

Just forgot about it and told myself that i have great friends who do respect me and didn't listen to what other people thought of me.

What happened when you did that?

I felt better.

What else do you wish you had done?

I did everything i wanted done.

White male in eleventh grade

Overall, what did you do that helped you the most?

Rationalized the situation. Most of, if not all of the cases, were just joking around. If there was any real tension, it was only slight. Many people are ignorant and close-minded about situations. If they are wrong about something or take their frustrations out on me, it's not my fault. I can only do my best to help them feel better or help correct them, but when it's out of my control I can only accept it.

What happened when you did that?

I felt better.

Female in eleventh grade, unknown race

Overall, what did you do that helped you the most?

Talking about it to my parents and friends.

What happened when you did that?

It helped me get over what had happened. It was just like a way to release any anger built up inside.

White male in eleventh grade

Overall, what did you do that helped you the most?

telling friends.

What happened when you did that?

they can comfort you.

which actions youth have used as well as the subsequent outcomes related to those actions. When students build on past success, they improve feelings of self-efficacy. We also encourage adults to use the Youth Voice Project data in supporting mistreated youth. Adults can encourage youth to use the self-actions identified as most helpful by the thousands of youth who took the survey. Adults can avoid advising the interventions that many youth said led to negative outcomes.

Four additional ways adults can help youth develop resiliency and respond productively to peer mistreatment include building positive narratives, cognitive restructuring through the use of filtering, teaching young people to solve problems, and giving positive feedback that emphasizes effort and actions over ability.

Building positive narratives

Our reactions to potentially traumatic life events are influenced significantly by the ways we think about and understand those events. Consider the media narratives about peer mistreatment to which young people are exposed. Clearly, the overwhelming majority of mistreated youth do not commit suicide as a result of bullying, yet teens hear repeatedly in the media about those who do. This implies that suicide is a frequent and perhaps even a normative response to bullying, which may lead teens to believe that negative outcomes are inevitable.

Stan observed another version of the same negative, hopeless narrative during a theater presentation for teens. Between skits, the director came to the front of the stage and told the audience, "I want you to remember that the emotional wounds that come from being bullied NEVER heal." When Stan later questioned the director about the wisdom of communicating this inaccurate and pessimistic statement, the director said that he wanted to get a message to bullying youth that they are likely to do real and lasting harm. Yet mistreated youth were also listening. What kind of future were they learning to expect?

Contrast this negativity with the message of the It Gets Better Project. Started by columnist and author Dan Savage, the purpose of the project is described on its Facebook page (www.facebook.com/itgetsbetterproject):

> The It Gets Better Project was created to show young LGBT people the levels of happiness, potential, and positivity their lives will reach—if they can just get through their teen years. The It Gets Better Project wants to remind teenagers in the LGBT community that they are not alone—and it WILL get better.

Although peer mistreatment can lead to negative outcomes, we need to communicate that many mistreated youth experience minimal long-term negative effects. It is also important that youth see mistreatment as a choice made by someone else, and assign total responsibility for the mean actions to the person or people who chose to use those negative actions. However, Stan learned many years ago from Claudia Jewett Jaratt, author of *Helping Children Cope with Separation and Loss* (1982), that it is not enough to say, "This wasn't your fault." Humans seek patterns and explanations for negative experiences. Jaratt teaches that young people need to find explanations that do not lead them to blame themselves and also do not fill them with hatred or bitterness toward others.

It is helpful for youth to create a narrative about the peer mistreatment that helps them understand what was done to them, what they felt when that happened, their role (if any) in what was done to them, how others at school feel about them, the positive steps they have already taken, the strength they used to take those steps, why others may choose mean actions, and what they can do to help themselves heal and abandon any self-blame, bitterness, or hate. These narratives are likely to lead to hope for the future.

Positive narratives include some understanding on the part of students of why others may have mistreated them. According to the work of David Yeager, Carol Dweck, and their colleagues, what adolescents believe about those who mistreat them matters. Adolescents who believe that individuals can change are less likely to seek revenge and more likely to forgive (Yeager, Trzesniewski, Tirri, Nokelainen, & Dweck, 2011). Forgiveness, in turn, promotes healing. Research suggests that it does not help targets of mistreatment to believe that their peers "did it on purpose in order to be mean" (Yeager, Miu, Powers, & Dweck, 2013). From our experience, youth often need help with this attribution process.

Some of the youth who participated in the Youth Voice Project survey seemed to come to a place of understanding without blaming themselves when they described the youth who mistreated them as having "acted in an immature way." It can be helpful for young people to see the people who mistreat them as immature, insecure, having had negative or destructive examples, or as lacking understanding about how to be a friend. With that said, our data suggest that this type of reframing is most likely to be effective for teens and less likely to help younger children.

We can help students realize that some people, at some points in their lives, choose to control or hurt others. This process can allow young people to let go of some or all of the hate and bitterness and move on. Helping youth let go is not the same as excusing mean actions or forcing mistreated youth to forgive. Specifically, adults can help youth develop positive narratives by listening; asking open-ended questions; focusing on goals, effective actions, and plans; encouraging journal writing, and helping youth identify their strengths and positive choices.

Cognitive restructuring: Using the concept of filtering

Cognitive restructuring is a process used in cognitive behavior therapy (CBT) that focuses on rearranging our thoughts to help us cope better with challenges. Cognitive restructuring has been defined in this way:

> CBT holds that most of our emotions and behaviors are the result of what we think or believe about ourselves, other people, and the world. These cognitions shape how we interpret and evaluate what happens to us, influence how we feel about it, and provide a guide to how we should respond. Unfortunately, sometimes our interpretations, evaluations, and underlying beliefs contain distortions, errors, or biases, or are not very useful or helpful. This results in unnecessary suffering and often causes us to react in ways that are not in our best interest. Cognitive restructuring is a set of techniques for becoming more aware of our thoughts and for modifying them when they are distorted or are not useful. This approach does not involve distorting reality in a positive direction or attempting to believe the

unbelievable. Rather, it uses reason and evidence to replace distorted thought patterns with more accurate, believable, and functional ones. (Bingelli, 2013)

In teaching about cognitive restructuring, we want to help youth to distinguish between constructive criticism, which can help them learn and grow, and destructive criticism, which has the potential to harm. Most important, we want to help youth filter out destructive criticism.

Stan discusses the concept of filtering with youth of all ages. He presents the following quote from our survey, which we have already mentioned: "A girl said that I was ugly, and every day I would cry, I wouldn't eat, I'd obsess over my weight." He asks students the sources of this young woman's emotional pain. Students identify three sources: what the other girl told her, what she told herself, and the larger culture's frequent message that being "ugly" or "beautiful" is more valued than kindness, creativity, generosity, persistence, or imagination.

Then Stan introduces the concept of filtering as "our ability to choose which ideas we will accept into our minds." He makes an analogy to filters in chemistry or engineering, which purify water by blocking contaminants. In the same way, the skill of filtering allows us to accept positive and constructive communications from peers while blocking potentially destructive communications.

To take the water filter analogy further, Stan asks students what conditions would stop a water filter from working. They respond that large quantities of contaminants could clog the filter. Similarly, he points out, many students can filter out mild or infrequent negative comments or actions. However, severe or frequent comments can overwhelm a person's capacity to filter them out. This does not mean that the concept of filtering is useless in more challenging situations, Stan tells students. Instead, it means that filtering is a shared responsibility, and students and teachers should take on the task of "cleaning" each other's filters on a regular basis by giving specific, positive, supportive feedback and by greeting, welcoming, spending enjoyable time together, befriending, and including others.

Teaching youth to filter is not a substitute for schoolwide efforts to reduce the frequency of negative peer-to-peer actions or to build peer inclusion and support. However, helping youth filter others' words and actions can help reduce the harm done by peer mistreatment, particularly during adolescence.

Teaching young people to solve problems

One way to build children's resiliency is to teach them how to solve problems. Teaching these skills is beneficial for all students. Developmental psychologist Myrna Shure has studied the ways young people think about their behavior since 1968. In fact, her work underlies most modern interventions focused on social and emotional learning. Her early research with clinical psychologist George Spivack (Shure & Spivack, 1980, 1982) identified a series of cognitive skills that help young people develop self-control and use positive behavior. Shure's work shows us that specific problem solving skills can be taught and that youth who learn those skills are likely to show durable improvements in behavior and learning. These reflective cognitive skills are particularly important during adolescence—a time when teenagers are overwhelmed with emotions and challenged with daily impulsive outbursts.

Three key skills are involved in interpersonal problem solving:

- Means-end thinking: Knowing how to set goals, identify and implement the steps that will take us to the goal, and realize that it takes time to reach goals.

- Weighing pros and cons: Looking at the positive and negative outcomes of a course of action before choosing it.

- Alternative solution thinking: Coming up with a wide range of strategies before beginning to evaluate any one strategy.

These skills make up the core of Shure's I Can Problem Solve (ICPS) curriculum (Shure, 2000, 2001a, 2001b) and are included in many other well-respected curricula that have built on her work, including the violence prevention program Second Step (Committee for Children, 1997). Together, these three types of thinking can be used to help youth solve social problems.

Developing problem-solving skills is best done through a mixture of curriculum lessons and in-the-moment interventions. The goal is for youth to learn concepts and skills before they need them. They are then prompted to use these skills in the moment.

Giving feedback that emphasizes effort over ability

Telling students how we feel about them or about their actions can have negative consequences. When we express disappointment, irritation, anger, or dislike for youth or their behaviors, they may respond with apathy or resistance. Youth may interpret these adult emotions as judgment or rejection and may react defensively to distance themselves from us or from learning.

Telling youth we are proud of them, that their actions make us happy, or that we like what they do can also have negative effects. Youth may interpret these statements as meaning that they have our approval or regard only as long as they do what we want. Youth may come to believe that they have an obligation to make us happy. Elementary school students may eagerly accept that obligation and seek to make adults happy by working hard and behaving well. However, as they become adolescents, those same students may choose to irritate adults by not doing their schoolwork and not behaving well.

Instead of encouraging youth to do things to please (or not displease) adults, we need to encourage youth to see the positive consequences that emerge from hard work and kind, inclusive behavior. We believe the internal joy of mastery and helping is a more effective and durable motivator for academic achievement and kind behavior than is pleasing adults.

We are guided in this topic by the work of Carol Dweck, who has spent her career studying how people think about their successes and failures. Dweck has written two books, *Self-Theories* (1999) and *Mindset* (2007), and dozens of articles on the topic. In a 2006 interview, she stated:

[There are] two mindsets that play important roles in people's success. In one, the fixed mindset, people believe that their talents and abilities are fixed traits. They have a certain amount and that's that; nothing can be done to change it. Many years of research have now shown that when people adopt the fixed mindset, it can limit their success. They become over-concerned with proving their talents and abilities, hiding deficiencies, and reacting defensively to mistakes or setbacks, because deficiencies and mistakes imply a (permanent) lack of talent or ability. People in this mindset will actually pass up important opportunities to learn and grow if there is a risk of unmasking weaknesses. This is not a recipe for success. . . . In the other mindset, the growth mindset, people believe that their talents and abilities can be developed through passion, education, and persistence. For them, it's not about looking smart or grooming their image. It's about a commitment to learning—taking informed risks and learning from the results, surrounding yourself with people who will challenge you to grow, looking frankly at your deficiencies and seeking to remedy them. Most great business leaders have had this mindset, because building and maintaining excellent organizations in the face of constant change requires it. (Visser, 2006)

Through decades of careful research, Dweck has documented that people who think that their abilities cause their successes also tend to believe that their failures are caused by a lack of ability. For example, people who explain their success in one academic area by thinking that they are good at history will also explain their failures in another academic area by thinking that they are not good at mathematics. Her research found consistently that when people decide that their failures are the result of a lack of ability, they become helpless and overwhelmed. On the other hand, when people identify their successes as having been caused by their own actions and choices, along with the support they have received from others, they are more likely to react to failure with creativity and determination. They are likely to find other ways to achieve their desired goals and to increase their efforts, rather than giving up.

We can apply Dweck's work to peer mistreatment in several key ways. First, we can discourage the use of labels such as *bully* and *victim*, which convey the message that people are unchangeable. Second, we can help youth learn new ways to respond to others. We can teach students to think of their brain as a muscle that strengthens with use every time they learn to respond differently (ideally, more effectively) during a social situation. We can use the same principle in helping students cope with traumatic experiences. We can emphasize that they can learn how to develop more effective coping strategies. Finally, we can give frequent and specific positive feedback focused on students' efforts, choice of strategies, and progress, instead of praising personality traits. Praising individual personality traits may lead students to feel discouraged and stuck when they experience failures—as though they can never change.

This form of feedback takes some practice and observational skills. For example, instead of saying, "You are really outgoing" or "I'm happy to see you trying to make friends," we can comment on a specific action and its accompanying natural consequence. We can say, for example, "I saw you reach out to your friends for support, and they spent time with you" or "I watched you support Molly after that happened and I could see the positive effect that had on her." When students make mistakes, we can reinforce that everyone makes mistakes and learning requires practice. If you have not already, we encourage you to investigate Dweck's work in more detail as it relates to optimizing students' outcomes.

CHAPTER 5

Peer Actions

No one is useless in this world who lightens the burdens of another.

—*Charles Dickens, Victorian novelist*

When any of us, at any age, witness mean behavior, we experience a dilemma about how to respond. Before we present our research findings on peer actions in detail, we invite you to think about how you would answer these questions:

- If you were in an abusive relationship, what would you want your friends to do?
- What would you hope your friends would not do?
- What would you REALLY not want your friends to do?

During workshops, Stan asks audiences of professionals in education and mental health these questions. Participants at one workshop said they would want friends to take these actions:

- Listen without judging me.
- Offer resources.
- Let me make my own choices.
- Help me have fun with them.
- Give me positive feedback about myself.

Participants said that they would hope their friends would *not* do the following:

- Tell everyone else about my situation.
- Judge me.
- Blame me for what is being done to me.
- Avoid me.

In this and other groups, participants responded that they would REALLY not want their friends to confront their abuser. Given the common advice provided to peer bystanders to "stand up to bullies," we wanted to learn whether mistreated youth agreed with adults about the risks of this response by their peers.

In the Youth Voice Project, we wanted to find out which actions of peer support and intervention actually help mistreated youth and which make things worse. Then we wanted to discover which peer actions were most common. To answer our questions, we presented mistreated youth with a list of possible peer actions, brainstormed with adult and youth input. We asked mistreated youth, "What did other students do about what was done to you?" and "What happened when they did that?" For each peer action, we asked mistreated youth to choose one of the following options: "no one did this," "other students did this and things got worse," "other students did this and things didn't change," or "other students did this and things got better." As with self-actions, we created a helpfulness score for each peer action. "Things got worse" was coded as negative 1, "nothing changed" was coded as 0, and "things got better" was coded as 1.

TYPES OF PEER ACTIONS

We separated the peer actions into several categories.

Support

Listened to me.

Spent time with me, sat with me, or hung out with me.

Gave me advice about what I should do.

Called me at home to encourage me.

Talked to me at school to encourage me.

Distraction

Helped me get away from situations where the behavior was going on.

Distracted the people who were treating me badly.

Help accessing adult support

Told an adult.

Helped me tell an adult.

Direct confrontation

Told the person to stop in a mean or angry way.

Asked the person to stop being mean to me in a friendly way.

Avoidance

Ignored what was going on.

Blame or ridicule

Blamed me for what was happening.

Made fun of me for asking for help or for being treated badly.

WHAT ARE THE MOST HELPFUL PEER ACTIONS?

The most helpful peer actions were those directed toward establishing a connection with mistreated students and helping them get away from the mistreatment (see Table 5.1). In fact, peer actions that provided connection and emotional support or distraction were rated by mistreated youth as more helpful than peer actions involving direct efforts to stop the mistreatment. Thus, approaches that encourage mentoring, inclusion, and emotional support are likely more promising than approaches that focus on teaching peers to "say no to bullying" or "stand up to bullies."

Table 5.1: Helpfulness of peer actions for all mistreated students (N=2,929)

	Helpfulness score
Spent time with me, sat with me, or hung out with me	.46
Talked to me at school to encourage me	.44
Helped me get away from situations where the behavior was going on	.40
Listened to me	.36
Gave me advice about what I should do	.36
Called me at home to encourage me	.34
Helped me tell an adult	.26
Distracted the people who were treating me badly	.25
Told an adult	.15
Asked the person to stop being mean to me in a friendly way	.11
Told the person to stop in a mean or angry way	.08
Ignored what was going on	−.13
Made fun of me for asking for help or for being treated badly	−.38
Blamed me for what was happening	−.39

In particular, the most helpful peer actions were "spent time with me," "talked to me at school to encourage me," and "helped me get away from situations where the behavior was going on." Interestingly, few grade level effects emerged for peer actions, indicating that we can encourage peers to use the most helpful actions of support and distraction in all grade levels.

Are peer actions or self-actions more likely to lead to positive outcomes for mistreated students? Overall, we found that supportive peer actions had a greater positive impact when compared with self-actions or adult actions. Clearly, youth have enormous potential to help protect other mistreated students from harm. Youth who are mistreated by their peers are likely to feel isolated and alone. When other peers connect with them and encourage them in meaningful ways, these young people are less likely to experience heightened emotional trauma related to the mistreatment. This is true even if a few peers continue to say or do mean things.

Not only do peers have the most potential to do good and promote positive outcomes, they also have the most power to do harm and promote negative outcomes. Overall, mistreated youth reported that, of all the actions they, their peers, and adults took, the most harmful actions were when their peers made fun of them or blamed them. Peers ignoring the situation was also more likely to make things worse than better for mistreated students, but to a lesser extent.

Elementary school students

Mistreated youth in elementary school reported that the most helpful peer actions focused on providing support, helping to access adult support, and distraction. For both males and females, supportive actions such as "talked to me at school to encourage me" and "spent time with me" were overwhelmingly helpful.

Table 5.2: Helpfulness of peer actions for elementary school males (N=150)

	Helpfulness score
Helped me tell an adult	.49
Talked to me at school to encourage me	.49
Helped me get away from situations where the behavior was going on	.45
Gave me advice about what I should do	.41
Listened to me	.40
Spent time with me, sat with me, or hung out with me	.37
Distracted the people who were treating me badly	.36
Told an adult	.24
Called me at home to encourage me	.13
Asked the person to stop being mean to me in a friendly way	.13
Told the person to stop in a mean or angry way	−.05
Ignored what was going on	−.18
Made fun of me for asking for help or for being treated badly	−.39
Blamed me for what was happening	−.48

Elementary school males found help accessing adult support one of the most helpful peer actions, whereas for females that action was a little further down the list (see Tables 5.2 and 5.3). Asking the mistreating student to stop, in either a friendly or a mean way, was not particularly helpful for either males or females in elementary school.

Table 5.3: Helpfulness of peer actions for elementary school females (N=168)

	Helpfulness score
Talked to me at school to encourage me	.49
Spent time with me, sat with me, or hung out with me	.46
Helped me get away from situations where the behavior was going on	.41
Helped me tell an adult	.34
Called me at home to encourage me	.33
Listened to me	.32
Gave me advice about what I should do	.31
Distracted the people who were treating me badly	.23
Told an adult	.23
Asked the person to stop being mean to me in a friendly way	−.03
Ignored what was going on	−.08
Told the person to stop in a mean or angry way	−.14
Made fun of me for asking for help or for being treated badly	−.50
Blamed me for what was happening	−.54

Table 5.4: Helpfulness of peer actions for middle school males (N=809)

	Helpfulness score
Talked to me at school to encourage me	.41
Spent time with me, sat with me, or hung out with me	.38
Helped me get away from situations where the behavior was going on	.34
Listened to me	.31
Distracted the people who were treating me badly	.28
Gave me advice about what I should do	.27
Called me at home to encourage me	.24
Helped me tell an adult	.23
Told an adult	.20
Told the person to stop in a mean or angry way	.10
Asked the person to stop being mean to me in a friendly way	.09
Ignored what was going on	−.11
Blamed me for what was happening	−.37
Made fun of me for asking for help or for being treated badly	−.44

Middle school students

For mistreated students in middle school, support and distraction were the most helpful peer actions. For both males and females, "talked to me at school to encourage me," "spent time with me," and "helped me get away from situations where the behavior was going on" were the most helpful peer actions. Females found "helped me to tell an adult" somewhat more helpful than did males (see Tables 5.4 and 5.5).

Table 5.5: Helpfulness of peer actions for middle school females (N=806)

	Helpfulness score
Spent time with me, sat with me, or hung out with me	.56
Talked to me at school to encourage me	.53
Helped me get away from situations where the behavior was going on	.50
Helped me tell an adult	.50
Called me at home to encourage me	.49
Gave me advice about what I should do	.45
Listened to me	.41
Distracted the people who were treating me badly	.36
Told an adult	.21
Asked the person to stop being mean to me in a friendly way	.16
Told the person to stop in a mean or angry way	.06
Ignored what was going on	−.12
Made fun of me for asking for help or for being treated badly	−.41
Blamed me for what was happening	−.52

Middle school females reported higher helpfulness scores for all positive peer actions and lower scores for all harmful peer actions than did males. This could be the result of cultural socialization of females to be more relational, thus making females more open than males to peer support and criticism. It is also possible that males who are mistreated also benefit from peer support but are less likely to report that they find it helpful. More research is needed to study these gender effects before drawing firm conclusions.

High school students

As is the case for middle school students, mistreated youth in high school reported that the most helpful peer actions focused on support and distraction. Males and females reported that "talked to me at school to encourage me" and "spent time with me" were the most helpful peer actions. "Helped me get away from situations where the behavior was going on" was also helpful (see Tables 5.6 and 5.7).

In contrast with elementary and middle school students, high school students reported that direct confrontation was helpful (though less helpful than support and distraction). Males found "told the person to stop in a mean or angry way" more helpful than "asked the person to stop in a friendly way." This pattern was reversed for females.

Like middle school students, high school females reported higher helpfulness scores for supportive actions and lower scores for harmful actions than did high school males.

Table 5.6: Helpfulness of peer actions for high school males (N=429)

	Helpfulness score
Talked to me at school to encourage me	.30
Spent time with me, sat with me, or hung out with me	.30
Listened to me	.27
Helped me get away from situations where the behavior was going on	.25
Gave me advice about what I should do	.24
Told the person to stop in a mean or angry way	.24
Called me at home to encourage me	.17
Asked the person to stop being mean to me in a friendly way	.09
Told an adult	.03
Distracted the people who were treating me badly	.00
Helped me tell an adult	.00
Ignored what was going on	−.06
Blamed me for what was happening	−.14
Made fun of me for asking for help or for being treated badly	−.23

Table 5.7: Helpfulness of peer actions for high school females (N=444)

	Helpfulness score
Spent time with me, sat with me, or hung out with me	.56
Talked to me at school to encourage me	.55
Gave me advice about what I should do	.50
Helped me get away from situations where the behavior was going on	.48
Called me at home to encourage me	.46
Listened to me	.41
Distracted the people who were treating me badly	.28
Helped me tell an adult	.26
Asked the person to stop being mean to me in a friendly way	.18
Told the person to stop in a mean or angry way	.13
Told an adult	.11
Ignored what was going on	–.21
Made fun of me for asking for help or for being treated badly	–.32

SUPPORT

The category of support included five peer actions: "listened to me"; "spent time with me, sat with me, or hung out with me"; "gave me advice about what I should do"; "talked to me at school to encourage me"; and "called me at home to encourage me." Overall, the most helpful of these actions were "spent time with me" and "talked to me at school to encourage me." We found no gender or grade level differences for "listened to me."

Spent time with me, sat with me, or hung out with me

Peers spending time with mistreated students was equally helpful for all grade levels. However, though this peer action was helpful for both genders, it was even more helpful for mistreated females than for mistreated males (see Table 5.8).

Talked to me at school to encourage me

Similar to the previous result, there were no grade level effects for "talked to me at school to encourage me." Although this peer action was helpful for all students,

Table 5.8: Gender effects for "spent time with me, sat with me, or hung out with me"

	Helpfulness score
All mistreated students	.46
Males	.35
Females	.53

Table 5.9: Gender effects for "talked to me at school to encourage me"

	Helpfulness score
All mistreated students	.44
Males	.40
Females	.52

it was even more helpful for mistreated females than for mistreated males (see Table 5.9).

Gave me advice about what I should do

There were both gender and grade level differences for giving advice. To understand these effects, we separated the data by grade level and then tested for gender effects within each grade level. Results showed that receiving advice was more helpful for males than for females in elementary school but more helpful for females than for males in middle and high school (see Table 5.10).

Called me at home to encourage me

Calling mistreated students at home to support them was helpful for both males and females, but was more helpful for mistreated females than for mistreated males (see Table 5.11). There was no grade level effect. This gender difference in favor of females is consistent with other research (e.g., Gilligan, 1982).

DISTRACTION

The category of distraction included two peer actions: "helped me get away from situations where the behavior was going on" and "distracted the people who were

Table 5.10: Gender and grade level effects for "gave me advice about what I should do"

	Helpfulness score
All mistreated students	.36
Elementary school males	.41
Elementary school females	.31
Middle school males	.27
Middle school females	.45
High school males	.24
High school females	.50

Table 5.11: Gender effects for "called me at home to encourage me"

	Helpfulness score
All mistreated students	.34
Males	.18
Females	.43

Table 5.12: Gender effects for "helped me get away from situations where the behavior was going on"

	Helpfulness score
All mistreated students	.35
Males	.46
Females	.35

treating me badly." Overall, helping mistreated students get away was one of the most helpful peer actions, whereas distracting the mistreater was slightly less helpful.

Helped me get away from situations where the behavior was going on

Helping mistreated students get away from situations where the behavior was going on was equally helpful for students of all grade levels and more helpful for mistreated males than for mistreated females (see Table 5.12).

Distracted the people who were treating me badly

Distracting the people who were treating students badly was more helpful for elementary and middle school students than for high school students. This action was helpful for mistreated males and even more helpful for mistreated females (see Table 5.13).

HELP ACCESSING ADULT SUPPORT

The category of help accessing adult support included two peer actions: "helped me tell an adult" and "told an adult." Overall, mistreated students reported better results when their peers helped them tell an adult than when their peers told an adult.

Table 5.13: Grade level and gender effects for "distracted the people who were treating me badly"

	Helpfulness score
All mistreated students	.25
Elementary school	.30
Middle school	.32
High school	.14
Males	.20
Females	.32

Helped me tell an adult

Helping mistreated students tell an adult was helpful for mistreated males and even more helpful for mistreated females. It was also more helpful for younger students than for older students. Though this action was very helpful for elementary school and still quite helpful for middle school students, it was just as likely to make things worse as to make things better for high school students (see Table 5.14).

This finding reinforces our concern that, too often, adults may not be responding in a helpful way to high school students' reports of peer mistreatment. As discussed in chapter 4, telling an adult at school was a helpful self-action for elementary school and middle school students but was about as likely to make things worse as to make them better for mistreated students in high school.

Told an adult

Like "helped me tell an adult," having peers tell an adult was more helpful for mistreated students in elementary and middle school than it was for mistreated students in high school. There were no gender effects (see Table 5.15).

DIRECT CONFRONTATION

Direct confrontation by peers was an important category, given the age-old advice for peers to stand up to the aggressor. Specifically, we wondered whether it made a difference how peers approached the person who was mistreating the student. In other words, would the outcome be the same if the peer "told the person to stop in a mean or angry way" or "asked the person to stop being mean in a friendly way?" To test this question, we included both responses in the category of direct confrontation.

Overall, results suggest that it does not matter how peers confront the student who is doing the mistreating—direct confrontation is not one of the most effective peer strategies in terms of leading to positive outcomes for mistreated students (see Table 5.16).

This difference between the two types of confrontation is not statistically significant. It is also important to recognize that youth told us that direct confrontation of

Table 5.14: Grade level and gender effects for "helped me tell an adult"	
	Helpfulness score
All mistreated students	.26
Males	.20
Females	.35
Elementary school	.41
Middle school	.31
High school	.07

Table 5.15: Grade level effects for "told an adult"	
	Helpfulness score
All mistreated students	.15
Elementary school	.19
Middle school	.20
High school	.01

Table 5.16: Helpfulness of direct confrontation by peers

	Helpfulness score
Told the person to stop in a mean or angry way	.08
Asked the person to stop being mean to me in a friendly way	.11

Table 5.17: Grade level effects for "told the person to stop in a mean or angry way"

	Helpfulness score
All mistreated students	.08
Elementary school	–.09
Middle school	.08
High school	.15

either type carries with it a risk of negative outcomes for both the mistreated student and for the peer bystander. Youth in our study reported both types of negative outcomes in their text responses. We found no gender or grade level effects for friendly confrontation, but we found that telling the person to stop in a mean or angry way was less helpful for younger students than for older students (see Table 5.17).

AVOIDANCE

The category of avoidance included one peer action: "ignored what was going on." Overall, this action led to things getting worse more often than it led to things getting better. We found no gender or grade level differences.

BLAME OR RIDICULE

The category of blame or ridicule included two peer actions: "blamed me for what was happening" and "made fun of me for asking for help or for being treated badly." Of all self-, peer-, and adult actions we asked about, blame and ridicule by peers had the most harmful effects on mistreated youth. We found no gender or grade level differences for "made fun of me for asking for help or for being treated badly" (see Table 5.18).

When peers blamed mistreated students for what was happening, things were more likely to get worse regardless of grade level. However, there were gender effects: Things were even more likely to get worse for mistreated females than for mistreated males.

Table 5.18: Gender effects for "blamed me for what was happening"

	Helpfulness score
All mistreated students	–.39
Males	–.33
Females	–.52

PREVALENCE OF PEER ACTIONS

In addition to establishing which peer actions were most and least helpful for mistreated students, we looked at what peers actually did most often in response to other students' peer mistreatment. We were pleased to find that a majority of mistreated students reported that peers supported them with helpful actions such as spending time with them, giving them advice, listening to them, and talking to them at school to encourage them (see Table 5.19).

However, around half of mistreated students reported that peers ignored the mistreatment. In addition, although the two most harmful peer actions ("made fun of me" and "blamed me") were used with the lowest frequencies, they were still reported by approximately one out of five mistreated students. Overall, more females than males reported that peers responded in helpful ways.

Elementary students

Elementary school males reported that their peers most often responded with actions of support and direct confrontation. The two most helpful actions, "talked to me at school to encourage me" and "helped me tell an adult," were used by peers only around a third of the time (see Table 5.20).

Elementary school females reported that peers most often responded with support, direct confrontation, and distraction (see Table 5.21). Although friendly direct confrontation was common for both males and females in elementary school, it was only relatively effective in terms of making things better for younger mistreated males. It was not effective for mistreated females in elementary school. Though this

Table 5.19: Prevalence and helpfulness of peer actions for all mistreated students (N=2,929)

	Prevalence rate	Helpfulness score
Spent time with me, sat with me, or hung out with me	61%	.46
Gave me advice about what I should do	59%	.36
Listened to me	54%	.36
Talked to me at school to encourage me	53%	.44
Ignored what was going on	51%	−.13
Helped me get away from situations where the behavior was going on	49%	.40
Asked the person to stop being mean to me in a friendly way	42%	.11
Distracted the people who were treating me badly	40%	.25
Told an adult	39%	.15
Helped me tell an adult	39%	.26
Called me at home to encourage me	39%	.34
Told the person to stop in a mean or angry way	35%	.08
Blamed me for what was happening	21%	−.39
Made fun of me for asking for help or for being treated badly	20%	−.38

Table 5.20: Prevalence and helpfulness scores for peer actions for elementary school males (N=150)

	Prevalence rate	Helpfulness score
Listened to me	47%	.40
Asked the person to stop being mean to me in a friendly way	41%	.13
Spent time with me, sat with me, or hung out with me	40%	.37
Told an adult	39%	.24
Helped me get away from situations where the behavior was going on	37%	.45
Gave me advice about what I should do	37%	.41
Ignored what was going on	37%	−.18
Talked to me at school to encourage me	34%	.49
Helped me tell an adult	30%	.49
Told the person to stop in a mean or angry way	29%	−.05
Distracted the people who were treating me badly	26%	.36
Made fun of me for asking for help or for being treated badly	21%	−.39
Blamed me for what was happening	19%	−.48
Called me at home to encourage me	16%	.13

peer action may not be harmful to mistreated elementary school students, we urge adults to stop suggesting direct confrontation as a primary response to peer mistreatment. Other peer actions have better outcomes for mistreated youth and come with less risk to the bystander.

Table 5.21: Prevalence and helpfulness scores of peer actions for elementary school females (N=168)

	Prevalence rate	Helpfulness score
Listened to me	64%	.32
Spent time with me, sat with me, or hung out with me	57%	.46
Gave me advice about what I should do	50%	.31
Talked to me at school to encourage me	48%	.49
Asked the person to stop being mean to me in a friendly way	46%	−.03
Helped me get away from situations where the behavior was going on	41%	.41
Ignored what was going on	38%	−.08
Told an adult	36%	.23
Helped me tell an adult	35%	.34
Told the person to stop in a mean or angry way	30%	−.14
Called me at home to encourage me	25%	.33
Distracted the people who were treating me badly	18%	.23
Made fun of me for asking for help or for being treated badly	17%	−.50
Blamed me for what was happening	16%	−.54

Table 5.22: Prevalence and helpfulness scores of peer actions for middle school males (N=809)

	Prevalence rate	Helpfulness score
Listened to me	42%	.31
Spent time with me, sat with me, or hung out with me	34%	.38
Ignored what was going on	34%	−.11
Gave me advice about what I should do	33%	.27
Asked the person to stop being mean to me in a friendly way	30%	.09
Talked to me at school to encourage me	27%	.41
Helped me get away from situations where the behavior was going on	27%	.34
Told the person to stop in a mean or angry way	27%	.10
Distracted the people who were treating me badly	20%	.28
Told an adult	20%	.20
Helped me tell an adult	19%	.23
Blamed me for what was happening	16%	−.37
Made fun of me for asking for help or for being treated badly	15%	−.44
Called me at home to encourage me	14%	.24

Middle school students

The two most common peer actions experienced by mistreated males and females in middle school were helpful actions of support. Around one-third of both males and females reported that peers ignored their mistreatment (see Tables 5.22 and 5.23).

Table 5.23: Prevalence and helpfulness of peer actions for middle school females (N=806)

	Prevalence rate	Helpfulness score
Listened to me	63%	.41
Spent time with me, sat with me, or hung out with me	56%	.56
Gave me advice about what I should do	49%	.45
Talked to me at school to encourage me	42%	.53
Asked the person to stop being mean to me in a friendly way	38%	.16
Helped me get away from situations where the behavior was going on	34%	.50
Ignored what was going on	33%	−.12
Told the person to stop in a mean or angry way	32%	.06
Called me at home to encourage me	27%	.49
Helped me tell an adult	24%	.50
Distracted the people who were treating me badly	22%	.36
Told an adult	22%	.21
Blamed me for what was happening	15%	−.52
Made fun of me for asking for help or for being treated badly	13%	−.41

Table 5.24: Prevalence and helpfulness scores of peer actions for high school males (N=429)

	Prevalence rate	Helpfulness score
Listened to me	45%	.27
Gave me advice about what I should do	39%	.24
Ignored what was going on	35%	−.06
Spent time with me, sat with me, or hung out with me	35%	.30
Talked to me at school to encourage me	31%	.30
Asked the person to stop being mean to me in a friendly way	31%	.09
Helped me get away from situations where the behavior was going on	26%	.25
Told the person to stop in a mean or angry way	26%	.24
Made fun of me for asking for help or for being treated badly	23%	−.23
Distracted the people who were treating me badly	22%	.00
Called me at home to encourage me	22%	.17
Blamed me for what was happening	22%	−.14
Told an adult	18%	.03
Helped me tell an adult	17%	.00

High school students

In high school, both males and females experienced support most often from their peers (see Tables 5.24 and 5.25). As is the case for middle school, slightly more than a third of mistreated high school students reported that their peers ignored what was going on. For high school males, the least common peer actions focused

Table 5.25: Prevalence and helpfulness scores of peer actions for high school females (N=444)

	Prevalence rate	Helpfulness score
Listened to me	69%	.41
Spent time with me, sat with me, or hung out with me	60%	.56
Gave me advice about what I should do	57%	.50
Talked to me at school to encourage me	46%	.55
Asked the person to stop being mean to me in a friendly way	41%	.18
Ignored what was going on	39%	−.21
Helped me get away from situations where the behavior was going on	36%	.48
Told the person to stop in a mean or angry way	35%	.13
Called me at home to encourage me	31%	.46
Distracted the people who were treating me badly	24%	.28
Helped me tell an adult	19%	.26
Blamed me for what was happening	19%	−.50
Told an adult	16%	.11
Made fun of me for asking for help or for being treated badly	15%	−.32

around help accessing adult support. These two actions were about as likely to make things better as they were to make them worse. For high school females, telling an adult was also one of the least common peer actions.

CONNECTION BETWEEN PEER ACTIONS AND TRAUMA LEVELS

Mistreated students who experienced moderate to very severe trauma were more likely to experience both the most helpful and the most harmful peer actions (see Table 5.26). Further study is needed to interpret this result.

ENCOURAGING HELPFUL PEER ACTIONS

Bystanders have heard a range of conflicting advice about what they should or should not do to help mistreated peers. Adults have advised bystanders to "stand up for mistreated youth," "say no to bullying," or "ignore it . . . it's not your problem." Many public statements advocate that concerned bystanders tell abusive youth to stop, either angrily or gently. However, according to the students we surveyed, we found that, generally speaking, this advice does not actually work to make things better for mistreated youth. In fact, not only is confrontation likely to be unsafe for bystanders, it is also not the most effective way to help mistreated youth.

Adults can encourage youth to be kind to and support mistreated peers in a number of ways. One important way to do this is to explicitly value all subgroups in a school. We discuss ways to build social equity in chapter 7. Other promising strategies include social norms interventions, using theater and video, using observational feedback, and employing a student leadership approach. In this chapter, we will also describe specific school programs to build positive peer behavior, including Wayne Elementary School's Doing Good Does Good program and James Bean Elementary School's Acts of Kindness Group.

Table 5.26: Prevalence and helpfulness scores of the most and least helpful peer actions separated by trauma level

	Helpfulness score	Mild trauma (N=1,351)	Moderate to very severe trauma (N=1,578)
Spent time with me, sat with me, or hung out with me	.46	42%	49%
Talked to me at school to encourage me	.44	33%	39%
Helped me get away from situations where the behavior was going on	.40	28%	35%
Ignored what was going on	−.13	33%	37%
Made fun of me for asking for help or for being treated badly	−.38	12%	21%
Blamed me for what was happening	−.39	14%	21%

YOUTH VOICES: PEER ACTIONS

We asked students three open-ended questions about peer actions:

- Overall, what did peers do that helped the most?
- What happened when they did that?
- What else do you wish other students had done?

The following responses are from students who reported mild trauma associated with their peer mistreatment.

Female in fifth grade, unknown race

Overall, what did other students do that helped the most?

friends were there for me through the whole process so i always had someone to talk to about what was happening.

What happened when they did that?

I had some one to talk with so things got a lot better after that.

White female in sixth grade

Overall, what did other students do that helped the most?

hung out with me so they cant hurt me when i have a friend with me.

What happened when they did that?

it helped and they left me alone.

What else do you wish other students had done?

nothing because everything helped that they did.

White female in seventh grade

Overall, what did other students do that helped the most?

came in with me to talk to the counselor.

What happened when they did that?

the bullying stopped.

African American female in seventh grade

Overall, what did other students do that helped the most?

My two bestfriends helped bring my confidence up because my feelings had been hurt.

What happened when they did that?

I felt alot better knowing that people cared and didn't listen to the rumors those girls were spreading around cause they weren't true.

What else do you wish other students had done?

Helped me tell an adult.

White male in seventh grade

Overall, what did other students do that helped the most?

hung out with me.

What happened when they did that?

i felt better.

White student in eighth grade, unknown gender

Overall, what did other students do that helped the most?

heard what i had to say and hugged me.

What happened when they did that?

i smiled.

White male in tenth grade

Overall, what did other students do that helped the most?

laugh with me about how stupid the situation was.

What happened when they did that?

it made the situation funny, not sad.

What else do you wish other students had done?

nothing.

Hispanic female in tenth grade

Overall, what did other students do that helped the most?

they were there for me and helped me through the situation.

What happened when they did that?

It helped me have more self confidence and know that i do have people that care for me.

Social norms interventions

The social norms approach is a data-driven, environmental approach that grew out of research conducted by Wesley Perkins and Alan Berkowitz (1986) at Hobart and William Smith College in the mid 1980s. The goal of social norms interventions is to reduce harmful behavior and increase positive behavior. The approach of social norming is consistent with one key observation: When people misperceive the behavior and attitudes of their peers, their behavior is likely to be influenced by that misperception. When we misperceive other people's attitudes and behaviors as more damaging and destructive than they really are, we are likely to change our own attitudes and behaviors to line up with the perceived actions of our peers. The solution to this problem is to educate people about the positive, genuine behaviors and attitudes of their peers. For example, students who report a misperception of higher than actual prevalence for alcohol use among other students also report more drinking themselves (Borsari & Carey, 2000; Lewis & Neighbors, 2004). We can correct misperceptions when we collect and disseminate credible, accurate information about peers' actions and beliefs.

The social norms approach has been effective and used primarily to reduce alcohol and tobacco use among teenagers. Stan was part of the Partnership for a Tobacco-Free Maine project in the 1990s, which worked to reduce teen tobacco use. As part of that project, he asked youth in fourth and fifth grades about their perceptions of how many teens and young adults in Maine smoked. The students confirmed the research in social norms by overestimating the proportion of youth who smoke, often by a large margin. In most of the discussions, large numbers of students said that more than half of young adults in Maine smoke, and often the estimates were higher than 75 percent. Stan took his video camera into a high school auditorium in which approximately 800 students were gathered for an assembly. As he panned the camera across the crowd of students, he asked everyone who had not smoked a cigarette in the past year to stand up. At that time, 28 percent of young adults in Maine smoked. Approximately three quarters of 800 students standing up in an auditorium provided a powerful visual, which was then shown to younger students. Often, students watching reacted with surprise followed by thoughtful silence. In one six-session sequence of lessons about tobacco, elementary age children told Stan that the video of the kids standing in the auditorium was the part of the program they remembered most. The campaign also used signs that said, "72 percent of Maine Teens Do NOT Smoke." This campaign was paired with pictures of youth who described why they chose not to smoke.

Social media are changing the landscape of social norms. In fact, researchers have found that norms related to alcohol use communicated through Facebook images (pictures of older teens drinking) and comments ("You were so drunk last night") influenced younger adolescents' attitudes toward alcohol use and actual alcohol use (Litt & Stock, 2011).

In applying the social norms approach to reducing peer mistreatment, we can expose youth to prosocial models of behavior that include supporting other students when they are mistreated, encouraging youth to invite others to their friendship groups, and reaching out to youth who may be alone. For example, we can highlight high-status teens on Facebook who use photos and postings to promote supportive, inclusive behavior for all. We can use engaging photographs and relevant postings to communicate prosocial normative attitudes about how we treat others.

Justin Patchin, at the University of Wisconsin-Eau Claire, and Sameer Hindu, of Florida Atlantic University, co-direct the Cyberbullying Research Center. On their website, Patchin (2012) wrote about the need to correct students' perceptions about cyberbullying:

> I ask [youth] to tell me what percent of students cyberbully others. Their estimates are all uniformly very high (70-80-90%). They are surprised when I tell them that the correct number is actually much lower than that—less than 10% have [cyber bullied others] in the previous 30 days. I was at a school this spring that had just collected data from its students about cyberbullying. I quickly skimmed through the handout that the principal gave me with a summary of the results and noticed that 9.5% of the students admitted that they had cyber bullied others. Yet when I asked the students during my presentation, they too estimated the number to be in the 80-90% range.

> Correcting the perceptions of youth about these facts is important because if they come to see a certain behavior as normative, they may feel free to engage in that behavior. Or they may feel pressure to "fit in" by doing what they think "everyone" else is doing. Well, the truth is that most students are not cyberbullying others. I tell teens that it is in their best interest to work to reduce the 10% number even more because, like them, the adults in their lives often see the behaviors of the 10% and assume that most young people must be behaving similarly. I mean, there is no shortage of examples in the morning paper or on the nightly news of teens getting into trouble for misusing technology. But these examples represent the exceptions rather than what is most often occurring.

> In the end, perceptions can be just as important as reality in terms of influencing behaviors. Which is why we need to work to educate teens and adults alike about what most youth are doing online, using valid and reliable data.

Successful social norms interventions rely on a set of core elements. These elements include collecting and presenting valid, reliable, and relevant data; avoiding negative messages that contradict positive youth norms; and using both quantitative and qualitative data.

If, after we have collected relevant data about peers' attitudes and behavior, peers' attitudes are significantly more positive than negative, we can disseminate that information in a variety of ways, using repetition and a variety of modalities to make the data memorable and meaningful. If our data show us that youth attitudes and behavior are mostly positive, communicating that data avoids the risks associated with adults telling teens what to think or do. If a significant percentage of peers' attitudes or behaviors are negative, we can use other strategies to change attitudes and behavior, rather than feeding back survey results that may actually have an unintended negative influence on behavior. Effective techniques to change perceptions include discussions to raise awareness, experiential activities to build

ONE SCHOOL'S STORY: DOING GOOD DOES GOOD

At Wayne Elementary School in Wayne, Maine, Stan implemented an intervention that students chose to call "Doing Good Does Good."* In this program, the school identified and tracked acts of student kindness by counting positive behavior slips. The school's community partners, who might be business owners or local individuals, pledged to contribute a small amount of money to an international aid organization for each act of student kindness schoolwide. As with a bike-a-thon, a sponsor might commit 10 cents. These small contributions, pledged by many people, made it easier to achieve one large donation.

At the beginning of the program, adults and youth got together to discuss the positive actions each group was planning and to thank each oth-er for the opportunity to help them make a difference. At the end of the project, the adult and youth partners got together again to review the students' positive actions and the adults' contributions. In this way, youth were able to see the direct and indirect effects of their own positive actions, both inside and outside the school. Adults had a way to contribute meaningfully to positive school climate, and the intervention built connections between the school and its broader community.

_____

*If you are implementing a similar model for reinforcing positive behavior at school, please let us know about it by emailing Stan Davis at stan@stopbullyingnow.com. We are accumulating information about this approach and would like to hear about your experiences.

empathy, and encouragement of high-status youth to convince their peers of the importance of adopting more constructive beliefs surrounding specific behaviors.

Social norms interventions are most effective when we mix numbers with personal stories to make the normative attitudes and behaviors more vivid and meaningful to students. This combined strategy appeals to both intellect and emotion. It is important to make sure that the personal stories we use represent behaviors that match our quantitative, numerical survey data. In other words, we should not use personal stories that represent the exception to the actual positive norm. For example, in our research, a few young people wrote us narratives in which they told someone to stop mistreating them and the person listened; however, the data clearly show that, on average, telling someone to stop the mistreatment is likely to lead to a negative outcome. In brief, because personal stories have such power to influence emotions, we should be careful to choose valid and reliable narratives.

Social norms interventions also show us that we should be careful to avoid scare tactics. When we make a behavior seem more prevalent than it actually is, we run the risk of convincing youth that most of their peers are using negative actions, thus unintentionally making the negative behaviors more likely.

It is best for schools to collect and use stories of their own students' positive actions. These narratives (with personal information removed) can be made into posters and spread throughout the school. Messages can be displayed on the walls during lunch, programmed into electronic signs, read during announcements, dramatized in skits, and/or sent home in parent newsletters. It is worth reiterating that it is important to remove all identifying information thoroughly when communicating students' stories to other students. This is true especially in small schools where it may be easier for students to identify the writer or the person who was mistreated if they read or hear a student account.

Using theater and student-created video to model positive peer actions

It can be powerful for youth to see their peers or older students acting out positive peer actions, especially when the actions portrayed were actually used at their own school. Plays or videos should focus only on kind actions that students can copy, omitting portrayal of mistreatment.

Playback Theater, a variant of improvisational theater, is one avenue for this intervention. In Playback Theater, actors portray a story or event from real life. Reba Short at the Children's Theater of Maine leads one exemplary intervention based on this concept. After training teenagers as actors, she goes with them to elementary schools. The teenage actors spend a day collecting stories of kindness from students they visit. In classroom workshops, they act out events from students' stories. At the end of the day, the actors gather all the students together to present selected acts of kindness they heard about throughout the day. Stan was present for one of these workshop/performance days. At the end of the day, he saw students sit quietly, apparently fascinated by seeing their own actions of kindness portrayed to them by trained actors, despite the fact that school staff had warned the actors that students at this particular school rarely sat still and focused during presentations. One student turned to Stan just after the performance and told him that she liked this play better than other plays she had seen about bullying because "I can *do* the things we just saw in this play."

Stan wrote in his book *Empowering Bystanders in Bullying Prevention* (Davis 2007a) about the James Bean Elementary School's tradition of having teams of graduating fifth graders work together to create legacy videos based on the life lessons they learned during their years at the school. Students had ownership over all steps of the process, including deciding on a theme, writing the script, and acting. The whole school, parents, and other adults in the community were invited to watch the videos.

Creating these videos helped youth examine their own thoughts, reflect on their values, and become more aware of their positive beliefs and actions. Younger children were influenced by the positive messages in the videos. Video is a powerful tool for creating a positive sense of "how we do things here."

There is one more benefit of student-created video: Young people who struggle socially or who have communication difficulties can produce articulate narratives that can change others' perceptions of them. Editing multiple takes can help young people effectively present their ideas. These changes may make it easier for students to value and pay attention to these peers.

Using observational feedback to encourage kind and inclusive behavior

In chapter 4, we discussed ways to help youth see their own positive effective actions and the outcomes of those actions. These same techniques can be used to encourage youth to support their peers.

Teachers can set aside a brief daily or weekly time for students to identify what they and their classmates have done to improve classroom climate, feelings of belonging, and learning for all and to examine the outcomes of those actions. In classrooms holding regularly scheduled class meetings, Friday's meeting could be dedicated to identifying the kind and helpful actions demonstrated by students in the class. This list of actions could then be reviewed in Monday's meeting to remind youth of which actions they found helpful. We encourage caring adults always to ask students not only about what they did, but also about what happened after they did that. This follow-up question helps youth internalize the value of kind actions by reflecting on the specific positive outcomes of those actions. When young people learn to see the effects of their positive actions, they grow in self-efficacy—that is, in the sense that their actions make a difference. They develop internal motivation to continue those positive actions.

We advise educators to use a process we call the "Empowerment Triangle" to teach young people the cognitive skills involved in this process. First, we can encourage youth to observe their own positive actions. We can teach this skill through specific observational feedback ("I noticed that you invited Sammie to sit at your table" or "I saw you encouraging Tameka"). We can also teach this skill through open-ended questions: "What did you just do?" Second, we can help young people see the outcome or effect of their positive actions. Again, this can be done through observational feedback ("When you invited Sammie to your table, she smiled" or "When you encouraged Tameka, she kept trying"). We can teach this skill through questions: "What happened after you invited Sammie to your table?" Third, we can ask students to reflect on how they feel about the outcome of their actions: "How do you feel about seeing that smile on her face?"

These three cognitive skills, used together, help youth create a path from action to outcome to their own decision to value the outcome they created. When young people follow these steps, they are more likely to continue positive actions. This empowerment process is illustrated in Figure 5.1.

Figure 5.1: Empowerment Triangle

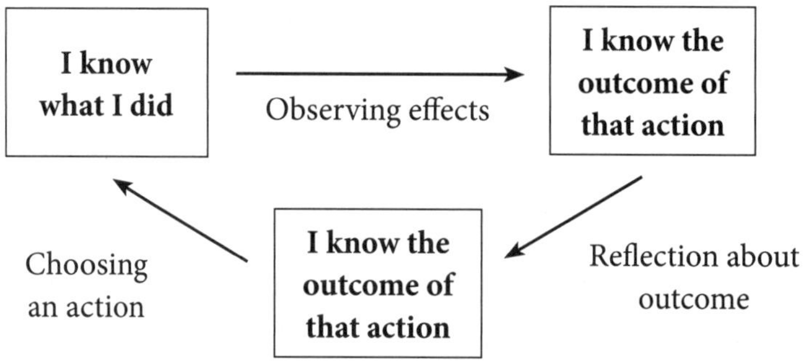

Build *intrinsic* motivation through feedback and questions.

ONE SCHOOL'S STORY: AN ACTS OF KINDNESS GROUP

At the James Bean Elementary School in Maine, Stan created an Acts of Kindness (AOK) group for students in grades 4 and 5. Any students could attend the group's weekly lunchtime meetings as long as they described an act of kindness they had done that week and the effects of that act. After each student told the group about his or her act of kindness, the AOK group spent the rest of the lunch/recess time eating lunch, playing games, making videos that talked about act of kindness, planning presentations for school assemblies, and supporting one another. This intervention was easy to implement and included a steadily growing group of fourth and fifth graders as the year progressed. It provided a safe haven at lunch and recess time for youth who might otherwise not be included or who might be teased and provided a chance for the school's many caring youth to interact in positive ways.

Pamela Orpinas and Arthur (Andy) Horne, coauthors of the 2006 book *Bullying Prevention: Creating a Positive School Climate and Developing Social Competence,* told us at a conference about a similar approach they used. At the beginning of the day, they asked each student to write down a kind action he or she planned to use during the day. At the end of the day, classmates were asked to identify what each student had done to be kind to others.

Christine Smaldone, a middle school teacher from Sudbury, Massachusetts, also shared with us a helpful activity she used in her classroom. At the beginning of each week, each student was randomly assigned another student to watch. She asked each student to observe the positive actions of the student they were assigned for a week and to write down specific positive things that person did and what happened when that person did those things. She prepared the students for this activity by discussing examples of kind behavior. At the end of the week, she asked each student to name the person they were observing and read one positive behavior. She had them describe what the person did and what effect the action had.

Many educators at schools use positive behavior slips to recognize and reinforce kind actions. These behavior slips are most effective if they identify a specific, positive action instead of just stating, "I caught someone carrying out an act of kindness." Older students benefit from writing a brief reflective statement on the slip as well, answering the question "What happened when I did that?" Behavior slips can be sent home and/or displayed in the hallway or classroom to build students' sense of positive peer norms.

On the basis of decades of research conducted by Edward Deci and colleagues, we discourage linking prizes or external rewards to positive behavior slips (for a review, see Deci, Koestner, & Ryan, 1999). The use of rewards for kind actions can encourage youth to complain when their kind actions do not lead to positive behavior slips. Prizes also encourage youth to see the purpose of kind behavior as earning rewards and recognition. As Deci and others have found, people who focus on rewards and recognition are likely to stop the behavior in question as soon as the reward is no longer available.

Our goal is to encourage youth to learn that their kind actions have positive effects on others and to take pleasure in their ability to help and support others. Robert Sapolsky describes the significance of helping others and seeing the result of your own kind actions in his 2004 book *Why Zebras Don't Get Ulcers:* "Often there is a staggering power in seeing the face that you have helped. In a world of stressful lack of control, an amazing source of control we all have is the ability to make the world a better place, one act at a time"(p. 407).

We are inspired by the Freerice website (http://freerice.com) to come up with a different way to use rewards. This website donates 10 grains of rice to the nonprofit United Nations World Food Programme for every correct answer to a posted question. Since the inception of this website, we have visited schools where students beg for time to practice for the SAT using this website. Using social psychological principles, the creators of the website encourage youth to form teams and pool their scores so they can track the contributions made by their teams as well as by themselves. By providing students with meaningful prosocial opportunities to help others, we can help them meet their basic needs in a constructive way. This website has stirred us to think about the value of altruistic, rather than selfish, rewards.

Student leadership programs

Student leadership programs have proven key in creating a sense of ownership and responsibility that empowers youth to change their social climate to one in which respect, kindness, and personal standards and character are the norm rather than the exception. Peer aggression, depression, cutting, and so on are symptoms of underlying issues such as a breakdown of positive leadership skills, ethics, school connectedness, and accountability. The student leadership approach helps students examine these issues from their own perspective and empowers them to support one another in creating positive change together.

One such program, Team LEAD in Valparaiso, Indiana, is a middle-school bystander leadership program for schools and communities based on student empowerment and broad-based education of staff and students. A key component of the program is student bystander leadership groups formatted as extracurricular clubs. The program promotes leadership, empathy, accountability and open discussion, building student resilience in the face of adversity through a focus on positive action and purpose.

As Valparaiso Community Schools educator and school climate coordinator Denise Koebcke describes, student leadership teams are formed around several basic strategies, which then become the foundation of the program: education, discussion forum, team building, and service/leadership opportunities. A focus on these four aspects addresses all the major protective factors: empathy, resilience, sense of belonging, and higher purpose. Most important, student leadership teams are inclusive—members are self-selected rather than teacher-selected—and meetings are held consistently during the school day once a week or once every two weeks. Adults support, facilitate, and encourage, but the ownership of the program belongs to the students. (For more information about Koebcke's innovative approaches, visit her website at bystanderlead.com.)

CHAPTER 6

Adult Actions

*The most basic and powerful way to connect to another person is to listen. . . .
A loving silence often has far more power to heal and to connect than the
most well-intentioned words.*

*—Rachel Naomi Remen, physician and founder of
the Institute for the Study of Health and Illness*

Emmy Werner became one of the pioneers in resiliency research in 1955. At that
time, she began a 40-year longitudinal study of an entire birth cohort of almost 700
children on the Hawaiian Island of Kauai (Werner & Smith, 1989). Werner found,
as expected, that some of the children in her study had every support needed to
start a good life. They had average or above-average abilities, stable and warm families, and homes that protected them from trauma. Also as expected, some children
began life without the same level of support and protection. Some of these children
had to deal with trauma, loss, addiction and other risk factors from a very early age.
These children at higher risk had less support and stability at home. Werner followed these "at-risk" children for 40 years. She found, as expected, that two-thirds
of these children who had experienced heightened risk factors went on to develop
intellectual and behavior problems by age 18. However, one-third of these at-risk
children grew into strong, capable, caring, successful adults despite their difficult
childhoods. Werner identified these youth as "resilient youth." Her work identified
the common protective factors in the lives of these resilient youth—the factors that
made their success more likely. Central to many of these children's success in life
were their positive connections with nonfamily adults. Since her landmark studies
highlighting the role of nonfamily adults in promoting resiliency, other researchers
have supported Werner's findings (e.g., Benard, 1991; Masten, 2001).

According to Ann Masten, Karin Best and Norman Garmezy (1990), resiliency
is "the process of, capacity for, or outcome of successful adaptation despite challenging or threatening circumstances" (p. 426). Researchers in child development
borrowed the word *resiliency* from the physical sciences, where it describes the
ability of an object to bounce back to its original shape and function after being hit or dropped. Some physical objects, like a china cup, will shatter if hit
by a hammer. Similarly, some youth seem to be severely damaged by negative
life events. Some objects, like a piece of soft wood or metal, will be dented or

deformed by a hammer blow. Similarly, some youth bear long-term effects, but not long-term impairment, from negative life events. Some objects, like a rubber ball, bounce back when dropped. Similarly, some young people experience few long-term negative effects from the same negative life events that may affect other youth severely. Unlike the characteristics of physical objects, it is now clear that human resiliency is not a fixed trait. Human beings can *become* more resilient when they develop skills and receive support from others in their lives.

Clearly, school staff have the potential to give that strengthening support and often play a very important role in the lives of their students. In the Youth Voice Project, we asked mistreated youth about what adults at school did in response to their peer mistreatment and what happened when adults did those things. We wanted to find out which adult responses to peer mistreatment were most helpful and which adult responses were most likely to make things worse.

For each adult action, we asked students to choose one of four responses: "adults didn't do this," "adults did this and things got worse," "adults did this and there was no change," or "adults did this and things got better." We again looked at average helpfulness scores for each adult action. As described previously, we coded "things got better" as a 1, nothing changed as 0, and things got worse as negative 1.

TYPES OF ADULT ACTIONS

After analyzing the data, we grouped adult actions into seven categories.

Support

Listened to me.

Gave me advice.

Follow-up

Checked in with me afterwards to see if the behavior stopped.

Kept up increased adult supervision for some time.

Class or school presentations

Talked about the behavior in class more than once.

Talked with the whole class or school about the behavior.

Brought in a speaker to talk with the whole class or school about the behavior.

Discipline

Said they would talk with the other student or students.

Used punishments for the other student(s).

Mediation

Sat down with me and the other student or students together.

Avoidance

Ignored what was going on.

Told me to solve the problem myself.

Blame

Told me that if I acted differently this wouldn't happen to me.

Told me to stop tattling.

WHAT ARE THE MOST HELPFUL ADULT ACTIONS?

When we assessed the adult actions that mistreated students told us were the most helpful, "listened to me" was reported as the most effective adult response to address peer mistreatment (see Table 6.1). Focused, genuine listening is a gift—a gift that can be used to help build connections, create more positive narratives, and instill hope. Past any refinements of technique is young people's need to be heard. However we listen to youth, we help them by doing so.

Mistreated youth told us that things were likely to get better when adults listened to them, gave them advice, and checked in with them afterwards to see if the behavior stopped. Overall, the only helpful categories of adult actions were support and follow-up. Class or school presentations, discipline, and mediation were about as likely to make things worse as they were to make them better. Avoidance and blame by adults were likely to worsen the situation.

Elementary school students

Mistreated males in elementary school reported that a wide range of adult actions led to positive outcomes. They identified support, mediation, and follow-up as

Table 6.1: Helpfulness of adult actions for all mistreated students (N=2,929)

	Helpfulness score
Listened to me	.38
Gave me advice	.34
Checked in with me afterwards to see if the behavior stopped	.31
Kept up increased adult supervision for some time	.13
Talked about the behavior in class more than once	.09
Said they would talk with the other student or students	.07
Sat down with me and the other student or students together	.06
Used punishments for the other student(s)	.06
Talked with the whole class or school about the behavior	.06
Brought in a speaker to talk with the whole class or school about the behavior	.02
Ignored what was going on	−.12
Told me that if I acted differently this wouldn't happen to me	−.14
Told me to solve the problem myself	−.17
Told me to stop tattling	−.29

the most helpful adult actions. Only one adult action consistently led to negative outcomes: "told me to stop tattling" (see Table 6.2). Females in elementary school found fewer adult actions helpful. They found support and follow-up to be the most helpful. Avoidance and blame were likely to lead to negative outcomes (see Table 6.3). Females reported higher helpfulness scores for the positive adult actions and lower helpfulness scores for the negative adult actions. Adult actions may have more potential for positive and negative impact with females; however, more research is needed to understand this pattern.

Middle school students

Mistreated youth in middle school reported that support and follow-up were the most helpful adult actions. Avoidance and blame were likely to lead to negative outcomes. Like those in elementary school, middle school females reported higher helpfulness scores for positive actions and lower helpfulness scores for negative actions, as compared with males. Tables 6.4 and 6.5 show the breakdown of student responses.

High school students

The number of helpful adult actions plummeted for mistreated students in high school. Whereas elementary and middle school students identified five to ten adult actions as helpful, high school students only identified three adult actions as helpful. Those three were "gave me advice," "checked in with me afterwards," and "listened to me."

Table 6.2: Helpfulness of adult actions for elementary school males (N=150)

	Helpfulness score
Gave me advice	.43
Listened to me	.40
Sat down with me and the other student or students together	.39
Checked in with me afterwards to see if the behavior stopped	.35
Brought in a speaker to talk with the whole class or school about the behavior	.33
Used punishments for the other student(s)	.31
Said they would talk with the other student or students	.31
Talked with the whole class or school about the behavior	.29
Talked about the behavior in class more than once	.28
Kept up increased adult supervision for some time	.21
Told me that if I acted differently this wouldn't happen to me	.05
Ignored what was going on	.05
Told me to solve the problem myself	.04
Told me to stop tattling	−.19

Table 6.3: Helpfulness of adult actions for elementary school females (N=168)

	Helpfulness score
Listened to me	.48
Checked in with me afterwards to see if the behavior stopped	.48
Gave me advice	.41
Kept up increased adult supervision for some time	.18
Sat down with me and the other student or students together	.18
Said they would talk with the other student or students	.08
Brought in a speaker to talk with the whole class or school about the behavior	.06
Used punishments for the other student(s)	.05
Talked with the whole class or school about the behavior	.05
Talked about the behavior in class more than once	.00
Ignored what was going on	−.03
Told me to solve the problem myself	−.11
Told me that if I acted differently this wouldn't happen to me	−.35
Told me to stop tattling	−.38

Table 6.4: Helpfulness of adult actions for middle school males (N=809)

	Helpfulness score
Listened to me	.35
Gave me advice	.28
Checked in with me afterwards to see if the behavior stopped	.24
Kept up increased adult supervision for some time	.14
Talked about the behavior in class more than once	.13
Brought in a speaker to talk with the whole class or school about the behavior	.12
Said they would talk with the other student or students	.11
Sat down with me and the other student or students together	.10
Used punishments for the other student(s)	.06
Talked with the whole class or school about the behavior	.06
Told me that if I acted differently this wouldn't happen to me	−.06
Ignored what was going on	−.19
Told me to solve the problem myself	−.21
Told me to stop tattling	−.33

Table 6.5: Helpfulness of adult actions for middle school females (N=806)

	Helpfulness score
Listened to me	.41
Checked in with me afterwards to see if the behavior stopped	.40
Gave me advice	.32
Kept up increased adult supervision for some time	.25
Talked about the behavior in class more than once	.12
Used punishments for the other student(s)	.11
Talked with the whole class or school about the behavior	.11
Sat down with me and the other student or students together	.07
Said they would talk with the other student or students	.06
Brought in a speaker to talk with the whole class or school about the behavior	−.01
Ignored what was going on	−.11
Told me to solve the problem myself	−.26
Told me that if I acted differently this wouldn't happen to me	−.27
Told me to stop tattling	−.37

For high school males, most adult actions led to things getting worse as often as they led to things getting better. Mediation and blame were likely to lead to negative outcomes (see Table 6.6). Females in high school had the longest list of adult actions that led to things getting worse. These actions included discipline, whole-class or whole-school interventions, blame, and avoidance (see Table 6.7). To a greater extent than in elementary or middle school, high school females reported higher helpfulness scores for positive actions and lower helpfulness scores for negative actions. Although not as extreme, this pattern was also found among high school males.

These results suggest that many adults working with high school students need to find more effective ways to address peer mistreatment and change negative behaviors. They also indicate that until we find ways to do that, it is crucial to offer support, reach out to students, build relationships, and follow up with mistreated youth.

SUPPORT

The category of support included two adult actions: "listened to me" and "gave me advice." These two adult actions were the most helpful to mistreated students. There were no gender or grade level differences for "gave me advice," whereas outcomes related to "listened to me" and adult follow-up varied according to students' gender and grade level. When youth described adult advice in their text responses, many described that they were given reassurance and encouragement rather than being told what they should do.

Table 6.6: Helpfulness of adult actions for high school males (N=429)

	Helpfulness score
Gave me advice	.30
Checked in with me afterwards to see if the behavior stopped	.23
Listened to me	.20
Talked about the behavior in class more than once	.08
Kept up increased adult supervision for some time	.05
Said they would talk with the other student or students	.01
Ignored what was going on	−.03
Brought in a speaker to talk with the whole class or school about the behavior	−.05
Used punishments for the other student(s)	−.07
Talked with the whole class or school about the behavior	−.07
Told me to solve the problem myself	−.08
Told me that if I acted differently this wouldn't happen to me	−.08
Sat down with me and the other student or students together	−.13
Told me to stop tattling	−.14

Table 6.7: Helpfulness of adult actions for high school females (N=444)

	Helpfulness score
Listened to me	.46
Gave me advice	.45
Checked in with me afterwards to see if the behavior stopped	.31
Talked with the whole class or school about the behavior	.08
Said they would talk with the other student or students	.01
Talked about the behavior in class more than once	.00
Kept up increased adult supervision for some time	−.01
Sat down with me and the other student or students together	−.02
Used punishments for the other student(s)	−.10
Brought in a speaker to talk with the whole class or school about the behavior	−.14
Told me that if I acted differently this wouldn't happen to me	−.17
Told me to solve the problem myself	−.21
Ignored what was going on	−.24
Told me to stop tattling	−.32

When adults at school listened to students about their peer mistreatment, things were likely to get better for youth in all grade levels and for both genders. However, though there were no gender differences among elementary or middle school students, listening was more helpful for high school females than for high school males (see Table 6.8).

For both peer and adult actions, listening to mistreated students was rated as among the most helpful behaviors. These are striking results because the supportive action of listening does not directly stop the mean behavior. However, being heard does help youth create internal narratives that make sense of negative events, reduce painful feelings, and reduce harm. In addition, listening builds positive connection and belonging.

FOLLOW-UP

The category of follow-up included two adult actions: "checked in with me afterwards to see if the behavior stopped" and "kept up increased adult supervision for some time." These two responses were rated overall as the third and fourth most helpful adult actions.

Checked in with me afterwards to see if the behavior stopped

It is important that we check back with youth over time to see if the problem is getting better or worse. Youth at all grade levels ranked this as a positive adult action, and it is a relatively easy action to use in a variety of situations.

When we check back over time, we communicate care and concern to children and youth. We also learn whether our actions have been helpful or not. We learn whether more active adult intervention is needed. If our initial attempts to help youth lead to things getting worse, these young people may not come to us for help a second time, and they may experience isolation and helplessness.

Although checking in with students afterwards was helpful for both males and females, it was more likely to lead to positive outcomes for males (see Table 6.9). There were no grade level differences.

Kept up increased adult supervision for some time

Keeping up increased adult supervision was helpful for mistreated youth in elementary and middle school, but it was about as likely to make things worse as to make them better for high school students (see Table 6.10).

Table 6.8: Grade level and gender effects for "listened to me"	Helpfulness score
All mistreated students	.38
High school females	.46
High school males	.20

Table 6.9: Gender effects for "checked in with me afterwards to see if the behavior stopped"	Helpfulness score
All mistreated students	.31
Males	.40
Females	.20

Table 6.10: Grade level effects for "kept up increased adult supervision for some time"	Helpfulness score
All mistreated students	.13
Elementary school	.20
Middle school	.20
High school	.02

Table 6.11: Grade level effects for "used punishments for the other student(s)"	Helpfulness score
All mistreated students	.06
Elementary school	.18
Middle school	.09
High school	−.08

CLASS OR SCHOOL PRESENTATIONS

The category of class or school presentations included three adult actions: "talked about the behavior in class more than once," "talked with the whole class or school about the behavior," and "brought in a speaker to talk with the whole class or school about the behavior." Overall, these three adult actions were about as likely to make things worse as to make them better. We did not find grade level or gender differences for any of these actions. We understand, however, that this is a very large and diverse category of adult actions, and our data do not give us enough information to describe which types of presentations are more or less effective. More research is needed in this area.

DISCIPLINE

The category of discipline included two adult actions: "said they would talk with the other student or students" and "used punishments for the other student(s)." Overall, these two adult actions were about as likely to make things worse as to make them better.

There were no grade level or gender differences for "said they would talk with the other student or students"; however, using punishments was more helpful for younger students than for older ones. Mistreated youth in elementary school identified this adult action as helpful, whereas middle school and high school students indicated that it was as likely to make things worse as to make them better (see Table 6.11). In addition, it should be noted that even within a grade range, the reported effectiveness of disciplinary interventions varied widely from school to school.

MEDIATION

The category of mediation included one adult action: "sat down with me and the other student or students together." Overall, this action was about as likely to make things worse as to make them better. As is the case for the use of punishments, the effectiveness of sitting down with the target and the other student(s) varied by grade level. Mistreated youth in elementary school identified this action as quite helpful, whereas middle school and high school students reported that this strategy was relatively ineffective for teenagers (see Table 6.12).

AVOIDANCE

The category of avoidance included two adult actions: "ignored what was going on" and "told me to solve the problem myself." Overall, both of these actions were likely to lead to negative outcomes for both males and females in all three grade levels.

BLAME

The category of blame included two adult actions: "told me that if I acted differently this wouldn't happen to me" and "told me to stop tattling." Overall, "told me to stop tattling" was the most harmful adult response to peer mistreatment, and "told me that if I acted differently this wouldn't happen to me" was likely to lead to negative outcomes. There were no gender or grade level differences for "told me to stop tattling," showing that this response is equally damaging for all grade levels.

The effectiveness of telling students that if they acted differently the mistreatment would not happen to them differed only by gender—not by students' grade level. Telling mistreated students that if they acted differently this wouldn't happen to them was about as likely to make things worse as it was to make things better for males, but it was likely to make things worse for females (see Table 6.13).

PREVALENCE OF ADULT ACTIONS

We investigated how often mistreated students reported that adults at school used each action. We were happy to find that the two most helpful adult actions were also the most common. Nearly 40 percent of students reported that adults also used the third most helpful action: "checked in with me afterwards" (see Table 6.14). However, we also found that nearly one in three mistreated students reported that adults avoided their mistreatment by ignoring it or telling them to solve the problem themselves. One in four youth told us that adults told them that if they acted differently this wouldn't happen to them and one in five reported that an adult told them to stop tattling.

Table 6.12: Grade level effects for "sat down with me and the other student or students together"

	Helpfulness score
All mistreated students	−.06
Elementary school	.26
Middle school	.09
High school	−.07

Table 6.13: Gender effects for "told me that if I acted differently this wouldn't happen to me"

	Helpfulness score
All mistreated students	−.14
Males	−.03
Females	−.27

Table 6.14: Prevalence and helpfulness of adult actions for all mistreated students (N=2,929)

	Prevalence rate	Helpfulness score
Listened to me	63%	.38
Gave me advice	53%	.34
Said they would talk with the other student or students	52%	.07
Checked in with me afterwards to see if the behavior stopped	39%	.31
Used punishments for the other student(s)	32%	.06
Sat down with me and the other student or students together	31%	.06
Ignored what was going on	30%	–.12
Told me to solve the problem myself	29%	–.17
Talked about the behavior in class more than once	26%	.09
Talked with the whole class or school about the behavior	26%	.06
Told me that if I acted differently this wouldn't happen to me	26%	–.14
Kept up increased adult supervision for some time	26%	.13
Told me to stop tattling	20%	–.29
Brought in a speaker to talk with the whole class or school about the behavior	16%	.02

Grade level differences

Overall, we found that adults were less responsive and supportive to students in middle and high school than to students in elementary school. For some of the most helpful strategies—including "listened to me," "gave me advice," "said they would talk with the other student or students," "checked in with me afterwards to see if the behavior stopped," and "sat down with me and the other student or students together"—there was a downward trend as students got older.

It is possible that adults in middle and high school are less likely to respond because they are less aware of the peer mistreatment. Alternatively, adults in middle and high school may actually be responding to mistreated students equally, yet youth may not perceive that these adults at school are supporting them. This latter interpretation is consistent with research documenting adolescents' difficulty reading others' facial expressions (Yurgelun-Todd, 2007). Regardless of the reasons for declining youth reports of adult support as they grow older, the data suggest an increasing need for adults working with adolescents to consciously communicate care and concern.

In general, younger students reported that adults at school were more involved in addressing peer mistreatment, in both positive and negative ways. Prevalence for all adult actions was lower for middle school students than for elementary school students, possibly because adults are less aware of the mistreatment. The results suggest a need to develop more effective ways to support older students around issues related to peer mistreatment. Given the current cultural barrier between youth and adults, it is important for adults at school to intentionally enhance efforts to communicate care and concern to teenagers.

Gender differences

More females than males reported positive adult actions at school in response to peer mistreatment. Although this does not surprise us, it is very important for adults to address this gender imbalance and actively reach out to males. It is essential for healthy development that males learn how to effectively solicit support. More females than males who were mistreated by their peers reported that adults listened to them and gave them advice. More males than females reported that adults at school told them to stop tattling, told them that if they acted differently this wouldn't happen to them, used punishment for the other student(s), kept up increased adult supervision for some time, and talked with the whole class or school about the behavior.

Both males and females in elementary school reported that adults most often used actions of support and discipline. More than half of mistreated males reported that adults listened to them, said they would talk with the other student or students, and gave them advice (see Table 6.15). More than half of mistreated females said adults listened to them and gave them advice (see Table 6.16).

Table 6.15: Prevalence and helpfulness scores of adult actions for elementary school males (N=150)

	Prevalence rate	Helpfulness score
Listened to me	60%	.40
Said they would talk with the other student or students	57%	.31
Gave me advice	50%	.43
Sat down with me and the other student or students together	38%	.39
Checked in with me afterwards to see if the behavior stopped	37%	.35
Used punishments for the other student(s)	34%	.31
Told me to solve the problem myself	33%	.04
Ignored what was going on	29%	.05
Told me that if I acted differently this wouldn't happen to me	29%	.05
Talked about the behavior in class more than once	27%	.28
Talked with the whole class or school about the behavior	27%	.29
Kept up increased adult supervision for some time	22%	.21
Told me to stop tattling	21%	−.19
Brought in a speaker to talk with the whole class or school about the behavior	18%	.33

Table 6.16: Prevalence and helpfulness scores of adult actions for elementary school females (N=168)

	Prevalence rate	Helpfulness score
Listened to me	66%	.48
Gave me advice	54%	.41
Said they would talk with the other student or students	46%	.08
Checked in with me afterwards to see if the behavior stopped	38%	.48
Sat down with me and the other student or students together	30%	.18
Told me to solve the problem myself	26%	–.11
Talked about the behavior in class more than once	26%	.00
Used punishments for the other student(s)	25%	.05
Talked with the whole class or school about the behavior	24%	.05
Kept up increased adult supervision for some time	23%	.18
Ignored what was going on	22%	–.03
Told me that if I acted differently this wouldn't happen to me	20%	–.35
Told me to stop tattling	15%	–.38
Brought in a speaker to talk with the whole class or school about the behavior	11%	.06

The most common adult actions experienced by males and females in middle school were actions of support and discipline. Less than a third of students reported that an adult used the helpful action of checking in with them afterwards to see if the behavior stopped. Nearly one-quarter of middle school students reported that an adult told them to solve the problem themselves—an action that was more likely to lead to negative outcomes. Approximately one-seventh of the students reported experiencing the most harmful adult action: "told me to stop tattling" (see Tables 6.17 and 6.18).

The two most helpful adult actions (listened to me and gave me advice) were also the two most commonly experienced by both males and females in high school. High school males reported a lower adult response rate for helpful actions than did any other group (see Table 6.19). Only around a third of high school males reported that adults listened to them or gave them advice, whereas more than 40 percent of females reported experiencing those helpful actions (see Table 6.20).

For males in high school, mediation was the most harmful adult action, and that response was used with 21 percent of mistreated students. For females, the most harmful adult action ("told me to stop tattling") was used with 13 percent of students, and the second most harmful adult action ("ignored what was going on") was used with 25 percent of mistreated students.

Table 6.17: Prevalence and helpfulness scores of adult actions for middle school males (N=809)

	Prevalence rate	Helpfulness score
Listened to me	47%	.35
Gave me advice	42%	.28
Said they would talk with the other student or students	40%	.11
Checked in with me afterwards to see if the behavior stopped	30%	.24
Used punishments for the other student(s)	28%	.06
Sat down with me and the other student or students together	24%	.10
Told me to solve the problem myself	23%	−.21
Ignored what was going on	22%	−.19
Told me that if I acted differently this wouldn't happen to me	22%	−.06
Kept up increased adult supervision for some time	22%	.14
Talked about the behavior in class more than once	21%	.13
Talked with the whole class or school about the behavior	21%	.06
Told me to stop tattling	16%	−.33
Brought in a speaker to talk with the whole class or school about the behavior	14%	.12

Table 6.18: Prevalence and helpfulness scores of adult actions for middle school females (N=806)

	Prevalence rate	Helpfulness score
Listened to me	53%	.41
Gave me advice	45%	.32
Said they would talk with the other student or students	43%	.06
Checked in with me afterwards to see if the behavior stopped	32%	.40
Sat down with me and the other student or students together	24%	.07
Ignored what was going on	24%	−.11
Used punishments for the other student(s)	23%	.11
Told me to solve the problem myself	23%	−.26
Talked about the behavior in class more than once	18%	.12
Talked with the whole class or school about the behavior	18%	.11
Told me that if I acted differently this wouldn't happen to me	18%	−.27
Kept up increased adult supervision for some time	18%	.25
Told me to stop tattling	14%	−.37
Brought in a speaker to talk with the whole class or school about the behavior	9%	−.01

Table 6.19: Prevalence and helpfulness scores of adult actions for high school males (N=429)

	Prevalence rate	Helpfulness score
Listened to me	36%	.20
Gave me advice	32%	.30
Ignored what was going on	30%	−.03
Said they would talk with the other student or students	27%	.01
Checked in with me afterwards to see if the behavior stopped	26%	.23
Told me that if I acted differently this wouldn't happen to me	24%	−.08
Used punishments for the other student(s)	23%	−.07
Told me to solve the problem myself	23%	−.08
Sat down with me and the other student or students together	21%	−.13
Talked with the whole class or school about the behavior	21%	−.07
Kept up increased adult supervision for some time	19%	.05
Told me to stop tattling	19%	.05
Talked about the behavior in class more than once	18%	.08
Brought in a speaker to talk with the whole class or school about the behavior	15%	−.05

Table 6.20: Prevalence and helpfulness of adult actions for high school females (N=444)

	Prevalence rate	Helpfulness score
Listened to me	46%	.46
Gave me advice	40%	.45
Said they would talk with the other student or students	32%	.31
Checked in with me afterwards to see if the behavior stopped	32%	.31
Ignored what was going on	25%	−.24
Sat down with me and the other student or students together	21%	−.02
Told me to solve the problem myself	21%	−.21
Told me that if I acted differently this wouldn't happen to me	19%	−.17
Used punishments for the other student(s)	18%	−.10
Kept up increased adult supervision for some time	17%	−.01
Talked about the behavior in class more than once	15%	.00
Talked with the whole class or school about the behavior	14%	.08
Told me to stop tattling	13%	−.32
Brought in a speaker to talk with the whole class or school about the behavior	11%	−.14

CONNECTION BETWEEN ADULT ACTIONS AND TRAUMA LEVELS

As is the case for peer actions, we found that mistreated students who experienced moderate to very severe trauma were more likely to experience both the most helpful and the most harmful adult actions (see Table 6.21).

We wanted to explore what actually happens when adults at school listen to mistreated students. To answer this question, we looked at the connection between adults' listening and students' trauma levels. We found that when adults at school listened to students who were mistreated by their peers and things got better, students reported lower levels of trauma associated with their peer mistreatment.

Our analysis also looked at the role of adults who listened in predicting students' trauma levels over and above students' gender, grade level, and frequency of both relational and physical mistreatment. Results showed that adults' listening to youth did explain a significant proportion of students' trauma levels, after controlling for gender, grade level, and frequency of peer mistreatment. In addition, results showed that it didn't matter which grade level students were in or whether they were male or female: When adults at school listened to them, they reported less trauma related to their peer mistreatment.

ENCOURAGING HELPFUL ADULT ACTIONS

Increasing positive adult actions can begin with data collection and education. One of the most important questions to ask students and staff is "What is this school doing to help all students feel welcome and belong?" When staff review answers to this question, they can make sure to continue the practices they are already using that are making a positive impact. In this context, it is helpful to take an in-depth look at specific techniques surrounding the most helpful and the least helpful adult actions: "listened to me" and "told me to stop tattling," respectively.

Table 6.21: Prevalence and helpfulness scores of the most and least helpful adult actions separated by trauma level

	Helpfulness score	Mild trauma (N=1,351)	Moderate to very severe trauma (N=1,578)
Listened to me	.38	42%	54%
Gave me advice	.34	36%	47%
Checked in with me afterwards to see if the behavior stopped	.31	26%	35%
Told me that if I acted differently this wouldn't happen to me	–.14	18%	24%
Told me to solve the problem myself	–.17	20%	27%
Told me to stop tattling	–.29	14%	18%

YOUTH VOICES: ADULT ACTIONS

We asked students three open-ended questions:

- Overall, what did adults do that helped the most?
- What happened when they did that?
- What else do you wish adults had done?

The following responses are from some of the students who reported mild trauma associated with peer mistreatment.

White female in fifth grade

Overall, what did adults do that helped the most?

they helped [me] know that it was not my fault and it made me feel better.

African-American male in sixth grade

Overall, what did adults do that helped the most?

keep a eye on that person.

What happened when they did that?

he acted different.

Other race female in sixth grade

Overall, what did adults do that helped the most?

told me that i was right she had no right to say that.

What happened when they did that?

it made me feel like i was right.

What else do you wish adults had done?

told me that this was going to end.

White female in seventh grade

Overall, what did adults do that helped the most?

The adult told me that i was worth more than what was happening.

What happened when they did that?

when the adult did that it made me feel better and i stoped worrying.

What else do you wish adults had done?

they did all they could to help.

Native American male in seventh grade

Overall, what did adults do that helped the most?

they made them stop.

White female in twelfth grade

Overall, what did adults do that helped the most?

They just let me vent and that made me feel better and have a cooler head about things. They also told me to talk to them if it got worse or if I thought I couldn't handle it on my own.

What happened when they did that?

It was just better for me and that they didn't get totally involved and talk to the other person without my permission about the certain subject.

White male in tenth grade:

Overall, what did adults do that helped the most?

Increased adult supervision.

What happened when they did that?

Things stopped.

Multiracial male in eleventh grade:

Overall, what did adults do that helped the most?

told me that life throws things at you that you may not like and when that happens, get help.

What happened when they did that?

I matured to the point where I now go get help when something is bothering me.

A closer look: Listened to me

Listening to youth shows them that we care about them. When we listen, we can help young people feel validated and identify solutions to problems. Our listening breaks down the loneliness of social isolation and gives youth a sense of belonging, value, and hope.

On one level, we all know how to listen. However, there is a distinct difference between just listening and truly hearing another person. Unfortunately, having someone turn off his or her phone, stop checking email, and listen to us fully can be a rare gift.

After reading over the Youth Voice Project results, Stan began observing his own behavior at the James Bean Elementary School. He noticed that he sometimes responded to students' reports of being mistreated by a peer by making sure he had the facts right and then dashing off to deal with the person who was teasing or threatening. He realized that he did not always take an extra few minutes to ask mistreated youth about their feelings and about what they needed to help them feel better. When he added these steps consistently to his personal protocol for responding to reports of mistreatment, youth responded positively. He found that they often did want to talk about how they were feeling or ask for help in rebuilding relationships or feeling less isolated. Sometimes they wanted help in figuring out whether or not what the other person said was true.

Listening doesn't have to take a long time. We can ask, "How do you feel about what happened?" and "What can I do to help?" Even in brief listening, it is important to be fully present in the conversation. We can do this by giving the person we are listening to our full attention (even if for only five minutes) and focusing on what the other person is saying to us rather than on the advice we want to give. Sometimes brief, focused listening is all that is possible. Sometimes we can take more time and subsequently are able to accomplish more.

It is often helpful to summarize what young people have told us to show them that we have heard and understand them. In doing so, we can begin building their sense of competency and resiliency by focusing our summary partly on their positive actions. For example, we can say, "You asked for help and kept asking until you got it," "You found a way to get away to a safer place," or "When one thing didn't work, you tried something else, which did work." By using this reflective strategy, we are helping youth build a narrative of strength instead helplessness.

It is also important to express gratitude when young people choose to bring their concerns to us. We should acknowledge that telling an adult requires courage and trust. Many youth have become convinced that telling adults about their concerns may be "tattling" and/or unwanted. For this reason, it is important to thank young people for sharing their thoughts and feelings with us.

It is a good idea to maintain a "notes of concern" box in the classroom or in the school. It is helpful to make this box do double duty as the place where youth place homework, absence slips, or other day-to-day written communications. Combining these functions allows youth to use the notes of concern box without peers' knowing that they are reporting a concern. Some schools use a website to allow the same type of reporting of concerns. It is important to let young people know that anonymous reports of mean peer behavior are welcome but that these anonymous reports will not lead directly to disciplinary responses in and of themselves. Rather, they will more likely lead to increased awareness and adult supervision, followed by further investigation if deemed appropriate.

Adults in a variety of roles at a school can connect with young people through listening. Teachers, paraprofessionals, custodians, secretaries, bus drivers, tutors, mentors, administrators, and many others can listen empathetically and supportively and help youth make sense of life events. Situations do exist that require a trained counselor, social worker, or psychologist. However, we can train and encourage all adults to listen well and help youth create positive inner narratives. Effective listening promotes independent thinking and autonomy, which is our ability to decide how we feel and what the best decision is for us. In respecting young people's autonomy, we may help them see that a wide range of feelings and decisions are open to them and nudge them toward decisions that are more likely to have positive outcomes. While doing so, we must maintain the awareness that we cannot make decisions for them.

When young people talk with us about negative events, we can help support their autonomy by using open-ended questions such as these:

- What happened?
- What happened next?
- How did you feel when . . . ?
- What do you think about what they said?
- What were you hoping would happen?
- What was that like for you?
- What did you think after that happened?
- What did you do that helped you the most?
- What helped you the last time someone . . . ?
- What do you think about what you did?
- What do you think you should do next?
- Why do you think they did that?

These and many other open-ended questions help young people explore their memories and feelings to make sense of negative events and to feel heard and understood. Asking open-ended questions shapes our own thinking as well, focusing us more on what the other person is thinking and feeling and less on ourselves.

In contrast, closed-ended questions such as "Are you mad?" or "Did you tell him to stop?" and statements such as "Don't let it bother you" and "You should tell adults every time" do not give young people the same freedom to tell us what they think or feel. Constructing and using closed-ended questions is likely to focus our attention on our own thoughts rather than on our students' thoughts and goals. In addition, closed-ended questions are often heard as criticism and blame by students.

Sometimes young people have trouble identifying feelings or thoughts. In that case, we can suggest four or five different feelings or thoughts they might be having and ask if any of those make sense. For example, we can say, "It seems to me that you might be angry or lonely, or you might be blaming yourself, or you might be thinking the person who hurt you is immature, or you might think this is silly." Statements like this help young people see that they can choose their own emotional response.

Respect for autonomy includes our willingness to keep encouraging young people after they make mistakes or choose negative actions. In many ways, helping young people with their feelings and behavior is the same as helping them learn math, science, or any other academic discipline. In both fields of endeavor, one-trial successes are rare. In both situations, youth may repeat the same mistake or make a different mistake a number of times. Our job, which can be difficult at times, is to start over with optimism and unconditional regard after each mistake or destructive choice to help youth understand the ineffectiveness of their negative actions or mistakes and to help them choose a different, more constructive path.

As we support young people's autonomy and decision making, we also must prevent them from doing things that harm themselves or others. When young people tell us that they have chosen, or will choose, harmful actions, we are obligated to do everything we can to stop them, including informing parents, increasing supervision, using consequences, and sometimes involving law enforcement.

We help young people grow into autonomous, resilient people when we help them discover for themselves their personal best pathways. We respect their autonomy when we ask them to examine their own feelings, past experiences, and goals.

A closer look: Told me to stop tattling

Students participating in the Youth Voice Project have helped us see that it is time to abandon the word *tattling* altogether and instead create school environments where youth are encouraged to share their concerns with adults. This idea echoes what most adults want in their workplaces: the opportunity to be heard when they have a concern.

A conceptual shift away from the concept of tattling has the power to challenge the teen code of silence and thus make it more likely that serious concerns will be shared with adults. This shift is especially important in view of our concerns about school shootings and school suicide, in which peers often have information that could prevent tragedy. The U. S. Secret Service's report about school shootings (Pollack, Modzeleski, & Rooney, 2008) emphasizes how crucial it is that youth feel welcomed to tell adults about their concerns:

> At least one other person had some type of knowledge of the attacker's plan in 81% of the incidents. More than one person had such knowledge in 59% of the incidents. Of those individuals who had prior knowledge, 93% were peers of the perpetrators. (p. 5)

ONE SCHOOL'S STORY: BLUE DOT CAMPAIGN

Here is an example of one school's intentional effort to listen more closely to students, as communicated to us by the teacher who initiated this program, Jerry Schrock. He explained that participating adults post a blue paper dot as a symbol that they are happy to listen, and that the use of the words Blue Dot *are a reference to the school's athletic history.*

Our Blue Dot Campaign has [focused on] a very simple message: at Mason High School [in Mason City, Ohio], our staff (teachers, teaching assistants, secretaries, counselors, administrators, etc.) care about our students. We don't claim to have all of the answers, but we will take the time to listen and try to help whenever we are needed.

Sometimes I am busy, and sometimes I don't see the importance of a child's needs at that very moment. We need to create a way for that child to know that there are some magic words that will grab my attention and show me that grading papers can wait. Those words are: "But Mr. Schrock, this is a Blue Dot Conversation." I know right then that it's time to close the gradebook and take the time to listen to a student who needs me. So far we have used the Blue Dot Campaign to change the culture in our building. We want our teachers to know that they are a source of support for our students, and we want our students to know that there are so many staff members in our school who love and are willing to help if they can.

Schrock went on to quote student statements about the Blue Dot Campaign from a public forum at his school:

"After I lost my best friend from suicide . . . the Blue Dot is one of the first things I turned to. It helped me in ways that I can't even describe. I mean, we're teenagers . . . we shouldn't have to deal with tragedies at this age. I mean, I know I have family at home but the Blue Dot to me means I have family at school also and that is a great feeling for me to know they will help when my real family isn't around." (16-year-old sophomore)

"Bullying will always be a reoccuring issue no matter how hard we try to end it. . . . The problem is that so many kids don't have the confidence to speak up to other people during difficult times. But, ever since the Blue Dot was created, it has served as a reminder that opening up to people is okay." (17-year-old senior)

In addition, the prevalence of telling students not to tattle reveals some of the unintended bias that school staff, as humans, demonstrate. Students mistreated around issues of sexual orientation and those with a physical disability and who get help from special education all reported disproportionately higher rates of being told by adults to stop tattling.

Educators have been teaching about the concept of tattling for years. Even today, one-fifth of mistreated students in the Youth Voice Project reported that adults responded to their reports of peer mistreatment by telling them not to tattle. Nearly half of youth who were told not to tattle said this adult action made things worse for them. Sixteen percent said this response made things better. This adult action had even worse outcomes than "told me that if I acted differently this wouldn't happen to me" and "told me to solve the problem myself."

To better understand students' perspectives, Stan interviewed youth leaders at a Vermont middle school in November 2010. He asked them, "How does it feel to be told not to tattle when you report a concern?" Their answers show the deep negative impact this response has on youth:

"It feels like they really don't care what you think."

"It feels like YOU did something wrong."

"Like you're unsupported."

"It makes you feel like you SHOULDN'T tell a teacher."

"Helpless."

"Like you deserved whatever happened to you."

"Like I'm not trustworthy."

"Unsafe."

"Worthless."

When mistreated youth are told not to tattle, they receive the message that they should not have asked for help, which subsequently can lead to feelings of damaged self-worth and loss of hope for the future.

Many educators attempt to teach students the distinction between telling and tattling. In curricula and books on this topic, the difference between telling and tattling is often defined in terms of intent and/or impact. When a child wants to get someone in trouble, that is tattling. When a child wants to help someone, that is telling. If no one is being hurt, that is tattling. If someone is being hurt, that is telling. These distinctions are taught repeatedly in lower grade classrooms across the United States and beyond. Books, games, and other educational materials reinforce the informal lessons that educators present to discourage tattling, thus defined.

Let us consider our lives as adults: Do we follow the same advice? If someone is driving unsafely on the highway and putting people's lives at risk, other drivers who call 911 are not asked about their motivations. Police don't wait to act until someone has been hurt. Adults experiencing sexual harassment are not denied the right to file a complaint if, out of anger, they wish to get the harasser in trouble. Youth are being taught a distinction between tattling and telling that is inconsistent with our lives as adults.

In addition, the distinction between tattling and telling is often taught to children too young to understand categorical thinking. These children simply don't understand the subtle differences in intent. Instead, they learn that telling adults about others' negative actions is sometimes wrong and may anger adults, as well as their peers.

Unfortunately, when we teach youth not to tattle, the underlying message becomes "We don't want to hear about your concerns." Certainly by middle school, this message has sunk in. Only 42 percent of the mistreated youth in the Youth Voice Project study who experienced moderate to severe trauma said they told an adult at school about the mean behavior that was interfering with their learning, sleeping, eating, or sense of safety. In related research, only about half of middle school students said they would tell adults if there was a threatened school shooting (Gaughan, Cerio, & Myers, 2001).

With regard to tattling, Margaret Berry Wilson (2011) writes:

> While perhaps well-intentioned, discouraging tattling creates more problems than it solves. It leads to a "culture of silence" in our schools and sends children disheartening and confusing messages: Adults say they care, but they won't listen to my problems. If I tell when someone does something bad, I'm being bad, too. I'm alone here; no one will help me.

> Such inadvertent but powerful messages clearly work against the culture of emotional and physical safety we want to establish for our children. Frequently we see reports of school officials who uncover bullying and learn that many students knew of prior incidents involving the same children. But the witnessing children told no one, and their silence emboldened those experimenting with bullying to go even further. We are often surprised by children's silence in these cases, but we shouldn't be. Often they're simply following the "no tattling" rule they learned at home or in school at a young age.

There are alternatives to telling youth not to tattle, but it is first important to note that educators and others teach the concept of tattling for some valid reasons:

- We want young people to learn to solve small problems themselves.
- We don't want to be interrupted by hearing about unimportant behavior.
- We don't want youth to try to get others in trouble unjustly by knowingly providing false reports of negative behaviors.
- We do not have the time or the resources to address all the concerns youth bring to us.

Each of these goals can be addressed without discouraging youth to tell adults about their concerns.

Teaching young people to solve small problems themselves is an important element of effective parenting and good teaching. The work of George Spivack and Myrna Shure (described in more detail in chapter 4) and others make two things clear: First, specific skills improve children's ability to solve problems. Second, young people benefit significantly when these skills are taught systematically. Like all good teaching, developing decision-making skills is best done through a mixture of curriculum lessons and in-the-moment interventions. The goal is for children and youth to learn concepts and skills before they need them. They are then prompted to use these skills in the moment.

Clearly, teachers need to limit trivial interruptions by students to teach effectively. Instead of taking time to teach the difference between tattling and telling, we recommend a different approach: defining, with student input, actions or concerns that educators should take disciplinary action about and those that staff should help youth deal with on their own.

When youth tell us, as Stan was often told on his elementary school playground, that peers are touching snow or have not fully zipped up their coats or are singing, there is no need to intervene. In situations that involve behaviors that are not against school rules and carry low potential for harm, we can thank students for telling us, using a neutral feeling tone, and then quickly change the subject, shifting the attention and speaking to other students. We can say, for example, "Thank you for telling me. You are all doing a *great* job of sharing the swings. Looks like you are having fun!" or "Thanks for letting me know. As I was saying, which math operation should we use to solve this problem?" This combination of brief acknowledgment and redirection takes very little time and strengthens the idea that we want to hear about students' concerns without reinforcing the behavior. In Stan's experience, and in the experience of others who have used this technique, this type of response often leads to dramatic reductions in the frequency of trivial reporting. The strategy is less likely to inadvertently reward trivial reporting through adult attention than an in-the-moment lesson in tattling versus telling.

Wilson (2011) writes about two similar strategies used to address trivial reporting:

> Be ready with respectful responses to "tattlers." Presume that a child's motivation for tattling is positive. Respond with a simple affirmation: "Oh, you're right. I did say that's how we should line up. I'll watch more carefully next time." Or say, "You really know our rules." If a child has reported a serious problem, be clear that you appreciate and will follow up on the information.

> Give students positive ways to get your attention. For students who seem to be seeking your attention through tattling, consider giving them a unique responsibility in the classroom, showcasing their talents at Morning Meetings, or writing them the occasional note letting them know you've seen their positive efforts or accomplishments.

If these strategies for discouraging trivial reporting do not work, discussions or even small consequences for interrupting instruction can be employed.

False reporting is a very real concern and should be addressed in a serious manner by adults. When someone falsely reports a serious negative action and we are able to determine that the reporter knew the report was false, we should follow up with consequences. It is important to remember, though, that actively discouraging false reporting is not the same as telling young people, "Don't tell me about things someone else did if all you want to do is get them in trouble." Getting in trouble for making poor choices is not necessarily an unwanted outcome and in fact can be a force for growth and positive change.

Clearly, school staff are stretched for time. However, listening to students' concerns can be brief, and it is important. Many student comments about positive adult responses focused on experiences related to being heard. Here are some student statements in response to the question "What did adults do that helped you the most?"

"They gave me helpful advice to ignore them."

"They gave me advice and watched out for me."

"They told me that it was OK and that they thought I was fine the way I was."

"Listened to me."

"I am very happy that my teacher would take the time to listen to my problem and help me solve it."

"They told me to just do not think that what they said was true."

"They were there for me and supported me through it."

These statements reinforce decades of research on resiliency that point to the power of small, brief expressions of concern and connection to protect against the harm that is often associated with peer mistreatment. Of course, we should stop mean behaviors when we can, but whether or not we can stop them, we can help students by listening to, encouraging, and supporting them.

CHAPTER 7

Social Equity

Education then, beyond all other devices of human origin, is the great equalizer of the conditions of men, the balance-wheel of the social machinery.

—Horace Mann, 19th-century American educational
reformist and politician

Because access to education is such a crucial requirement for life success, it is essential that we examine our practices carefully to assure that subgroups are treated fairly. We believe that most educators want all students to succeed in school and in life, have chosen their profession to help youth, and approach teaching without conscious bias. Yet we are human and live in an imperfect society, so it is difficult to avoid subconscious bias or discrimination unless we examine our own actions in an ongoing, careful manner that includes gathering data about equity in our schools.

Differential connectedness to school and to teachers is one concrete indicator of equity or inequity that is easily measured and relatively easily remediated. Later in this chapter, we will highlight the successful work of one school in Wyoming to improve school connection variables for youth of color.

Past studies have examined the use of school discipline with different subgroups. Skiba, Michael, Nardo, and Peterson (2002) examined patterns of school discipline by race. The striking findings of this study are illustrated in Figure 7.1.

Skiba and colleagues' study results show that African American youth, as compared with White youth, were more likely to be suspended and expelled for four behaviors: disrespect, excessive noise, threat, and loitering. What we find striking about these behaviors is how poorly defined they are. The absence of objective criteria for deciding whether these four rules have been broken makes it possible, even likely, that identical behaviors by White and African American youth could be judged differently. This differential rate of suspension is especially unacceptable because of the large body of research that shows the results of suspension. The national High School and Beyond Survey (Ekstrom, Goertz, Pollack, & Rock, 1986) found that 31 percent of sophomores who dropped out of

Figure 7.1: Disproportionality in school discipline at the national level: 1972, 2000, 2003

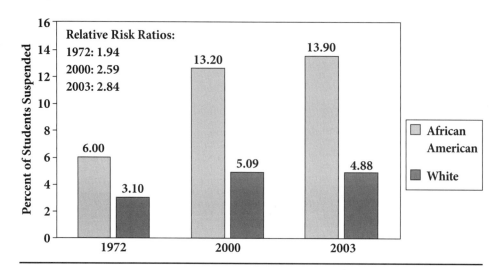

school had been suspended, whereas only 10 percent of their peers who stayed in school had been suspended.

Skiba et al. (2002) address the question that may be on some people's minds: Is this higher per capita rate of suspension due to more negative behavior by African American youth? The study found no reason to believe that African American youth misbehave more than White youth. In fact, they found a differential pattern of disciplinary referrals for more subjective behaviors among African American students compared with their peers.

A similar pattern of unequal treatment among nonheterosexual adolescents in school and in the community was documented in the National Longitudinal Study of Adolescent Health. In this study, Kathryn Himmelstein and Hannah Brückner (2011) studied 15,000 middle and high school students for seven years. They found that even when controlling for demographic variables and misbehaviors, lesbian, gay, and bisexual (LGB) adolescents were 40 percent more likely than other teens to be punished by school authorities, police, and the courts. Virtually all types of punishment, including expulsion, arrest, convictions, and police stops, were more frequent among LGB youth. Teens who reported feelings of attraction to members of the same sex, regardless of their self-identification, were more likely than other adolescents to be expelled from school. Nonheterosexual girls were particularly at risk.

CHARACTERISTICS OF MISTREATED STUDENTS

Results from the Youth Voice Project also showed that peers and adults at school treated youth belonging to different subgroups differently. Specifically, we explored the following student demographics as possible predictors of group membership:

- Gender

- Physical disability
- Special education status
- Race (White or of color)
- Socioeconomic status (receiving free or reduced lunch)

Peer mistreatment

Do certain student demographics increase or decrease the likelihood that students will be relationally and physically mistreated? To answer this question, we conducted two logistic regressions—one model predicting how likely it was for students to be regularly excluded by their peers (at least twice a month) and one model predicting how likely it was for students to be physically mistreated by their peers (at least twice a month).

Which student demographics predict increased relational peer mistreatment?

We found that females were .84 times more likely to be relationally mistreated than males. We found that the odds of a student *with* a physical disability were 1.94 times greater than the odds of a student *without* a physical disability to be relationally mistreated (e.g., excluded) by his or her peers. Similarly, students receiving special education services were 1.66 times more likely to be relationally mistreated, compared to their peers who did not receive special education services. The odds of a White student being relationally mistreated were 1.19 times greater than the odds of a child of color (e.g., African American or Hispanic American) being relationally mistreated. Students' socioeconomic status did not predict their likelihood of being relationally mistreated by their peers.

Which student demographics predict increased physical peer mistreatment?

Males were 2.22 times more likely to be physically mistreated by their peers, compared to females. Students with a physical disability were 2.45 times more likely to be physically mistreated, compared to students without a physical disability. And students receiving special education services were 1.77 times more likely to be physically mistreated by their peers. Students' socioeconomic status and race did not predict their odds of being physically mistreated by their peers.

Trauma

We asked whether some students are more likely to experience increased trauma (i.e., moderate to very severe versus mild) related to their peer mistreatment. To answer this question, we conducted a logistic regression model to see which student characteristics predicted moderate to very severe trauma levels (compared to mild trauma levels) related to peer mistreatment. We found that females were 1.87 times more likely to experience moderate to very severe trauma as a result of their peer mistreatment, compared to males. Mirroring this pattern, students with a physical disability were 1.80 times more likely and students receiving special education services were 1.63 times more likely to experience moderate to very severe trauma. Students' socioeconomic status and race were not related to their trauma levels.

Demographics and school connection variables

We found that males, students with a physical disability, students who receive special education services, students who receive or are eligible for free or reduced lunch, and students of color scored lower than the general population on one or more school connection variables (see Table 7.1). Males reported feeling less a part of school and less close to adults at school than did females, but they reported feeling about the same amount of value and respect at school. Students with a physical disability reported lower scores than the general population on all three connection variables. Students who receive special education services reported feeling less a part of school and less valued and respected at school than their peers, but they reported feeling closer to adults at school. Students who receive or are eligible for free or reduced lunch reported feeling less valued and respected at school but more like a part of their school. Although White students reported higher scores on all three school connection variables, students of color reported that they felt significantly less valued and respected at school.

HOW DO ADULTS AND PEERS RESPOND TO STUDENT SUBGROUPS?

To gauge how adults responded to youth in different groups, we tested the relationship between group membership and the four adult actions youth said were most likely to make things better: "listened to me," "gave me advice," "checked in with me afterwards to see if the behavior stopped," and "kept up increased supervision for some time." We also tested the relationship between group membership and the four adult responses that youth in our survey said were most likely to make things worse: "ignored what was going on," "told me that if I acted differently this wouldn't happen to me," "told me to solve the problem myself," and "told me to stop tattling."

Table 7.1: Demographic comparison of school connection variables

	I feel like I am part of this school	I feel valued and respected at school	I feel close to adults at my school
All mistreated students	3.72	3.20	3.21
Males	3.70	3.23	3.15
Females	3.81	3.22	3.30
Students with a physical disability	3.47	2.86	3.13
Students who get help from special education	3.49	3.02	3.44
Receive or are eligible for free or reduced lunch	3.78	3.08	3.20
White students	3.88	3.29	3.38
Students of color	3.70	3.12	3.19

Note: 1=NO!, 3=Unsure, 5=YES!

We also looked at peer responses to each subgroup. Again, we looked at the four peer actions mistreated youth said were most likely to make things better: "spent time with me," "sat with me or hung out with me," "talked to me at school to encourage me," "helped me get away from situations where the behavior was going on," and "listened to me." We also looked at the relationship between group membership and the three peer actions mistreated youth said were most likely to make things worse: "ignored what was going on," "made fun of me for asking for help or for being treated badly," and "blamed me for what was happening."

The prevalence of positive peer and adult actions varies from group to group. Students mistreated around sexual orientation, students with a physical disability, students who receive special education services, and students of color were all more likely to have peers ignore what was going on, make fun of them for asking for help or for being treated badly, and blame them for what was happening. Perhaps even more concerning is the fact that these same minority groups were more likely to have adults ignore what was going on, tell them that if they acted differently this wouldn't happen to them, tell them to solve the problem themselves, and tell them to stop tattling.

Youth who receive help from special education or have physical disabilities and young people who are mistreated with a focus on sexual orientation reported higher frequencies of mistreatment than other youth in our study. These same groups of young people, reported higher rates of trauma associated with their peer mistreatment. Clearly, these groups of young people need more support from adults at school than do their peers. Yet we were concerned to find that youth in these groups also reported that adults at school were more likely to respond to their peer mistreatment with negative actions, compared to their peers. This pattern makes it plain that our efforts to change assumptions and reduce bias cannot be limited to discussions with students alone but also need to include ongoing work with adults in schools to address potential negative assumptions about student subgroups.

Reducing bias can be difficult in a time when the concept of diversity education can trigger heated political discourse. Stan was moved by a discussion he had with one teacher after a 2012 workshop. She began the discussion by telling him that she disagreed with some of what he said about supporting nonheterosexual youth. She told him that, for religious reasons, she did not want to be told that she has to accept "the gay lifestyle" as a positive one.

As she and Stan talked, they looked for areas of agreement. They found complete agreement in two key statements, which helped this teacher see what she could do:

- It is every educator's job to welcome, care about, and support every student, no matter whom that student loves or how the student lives.

- It is every educator's job to insist that others at school treat each student with respect and in such a way that supports each student's dignity as a person.

The students in our survey population have shown us that we have not yet reached these core goals. They have told us that we have more work to do, especially with youth in special education, youth with disabilities, youth of color, and youth who are mistreated around issues related to sexual orientation. We believe that we can make progress in these areas.

SEXUAL ORIENTATION

We did not ask students to indicate their sexual orientation. We did, however, ask students which issues their mistreatment focused on. Of all mistreated students, 11 percent reported being mistreated around sexual orientation. Students who were mistreated by their peers around issues related to sexual orientation were likely to report higher trauma levels.

As Figure 7.2 shows, students who were mistreated around issues related to sexual orientation were much more likely to report severe and very severe trauma, compared to their peers who were mistreated around other issues not related to sexual orientation. This increase in reported trauma was true among students in all three grade levels. Being mistreated around sexual orientation was particularly harmful for younger students in terms of being related to increased trauma levels. Clearly, we should be especially vigilant about peer mistreatment focused on sexual orientation and about the needs of GLBT youth and youth whose gender expression is outside our culture's fairly narrow norms.

Youth who were mistreated around sexual orientation were no more or less likely to experience the four most helpful peer actions. These youth were,

Figure 7.2: Mistreatment around sexual orientation versus other issues related to trauma

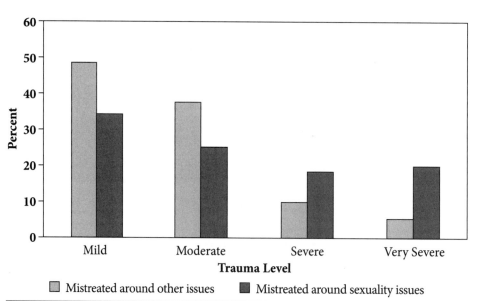

Table 7.2: Prevalence of peer actions toward students mistreated around sexual orientation

	Overall helpfulness score	Prevalence with students mistreated around sexual orientation	Prevalence with students mistreated around other issues
Positive peer actions			
Spent time with me, sat with me, or hung out with me	.46	55%	54%
Talked to me at school to encourage me	.44	45%	43%
Helped me get away from the situations where the behavior was going on	.40	39%	38%
Listened to me	.36	63%	63%
Negative peer actions			
Ignored what was going on	−.13	48%	41%
Made fun of me for asking for help or for being treated badly	−.38	33%	19%
Blamed me for what was happening	−.39	33%	20%

however, more likely to report being ignored, blamed, and made fun of by peers.

Results showed that students who were mistreated around sexual orientation were less likely to receive support from adults at school but more likely to have adults follow up with them later. These students were also more likely to report experiencing all of the four most harmful adult actions (see Table 7.3).

Table 7.3: Prevalence of adult actions toward students mistreated around sexual orientation

	Overall helpfulness score	Prevalence with students mistreated around sexual orientation	Prevalence with students mistreated around other issues
Positive adult actions			
Listened to me	.38	55%	59%
Gave me advice	.34	45%	50%
Checked in with me afterwards to see if the behavior stopped	.31	42%	37%
Kept up increased adult supervision for some time	.13	32%	24%
Negative adult actions			
Ignored what was going on	−.12	40%	29%
Told me that if I acted differently this wouldn't happen to me	−.14	33%	25%
Told me to solve the problem myself	−.17	33%	28%
Told me to stop tattling	−.29	30%	18%

These results show a need for a change in adult attitudes and behavior—in particular, how adults at school respond to youth who are mistreated around issues related to sexual orientation. We also found that mistreatment focused on sexual orientation led to more negative student outcomes (i.e., increased trauma levels) compared with other types of mistreatment. We believe these findings emphasize the need for collaboration between schools and such organizations as the Gay Lesbian Straight Education Network (GLSEN), to help educators respond more effectively to homophobic peer mistreatment directed toward both GLBT and straight youth.

GENDER

Males and females were equally likely to report experiencing relational mistreatment by their peers, although males reported a higher rate of physical mistreatment than females. Females reported higher trauma levels related to their peer mistreatment in all three grade levels. Mistreated females were more likely to experience supportive peer actions and less likely to experience harmful peer actions than were males (see Table 7.4). Adults too were more positive and supportive toward mistreated females and more negative and blaming toward mistreated males. However, adults checked in with males and females at about the same rate, and males reported that adults more often kept up with increased supervision (see Table 7.5).

PHYSICAL DISABILITY

Students with a physical disability reported proportionately more mistreatment than students without a physical disability. Such students also reported higher trauma levels related to their peer mistreatment. These increased trauma levels were evident for both boys and girls in all three grade levels.

Table 7.4: Prevalence of peer actions toward males and females

	Overall helpfulness score	Prevalence with males	Prevalence with females
Positive peer actions			
Spent time with me, sat with me, or hung out with me	.46	43%	65%
Talked to me at school to encourage me	.44	35%	51%
Helped me get away from the situations where the behavior was going on	.40	34%	42%
Listened to me	.36	53%	73%
Negative peer actions			
Ignored what was going on	−.13	42%	41%
Made fun of me for asking for help or for being treated badly	−.38	23%	16%
Blamed me for what was happening	−.39	23%	19%

Table 7.5: Prevalence of adult actions toward males and females

	Overall helpfulness score	Prevalence with males	Prevalence with females
Positive adult actions			
Listened to me	.38	55%	62%
Gave me advice	.34	48%	53%
Checked in with me afterwards to see if the behavior stopped	.31	37%	39%
Kept up increased adult supervision for some time	.13	27%	22%
Negative adult actions			
Ignored what was going on	−.12	32%	29%
Told me that if I acted differently this wouldn't happen to me	−.14	29%	22%
Told me to solve the problem myself	−.17	30%	27%
Told me to stop tattling	−.29	22%	17%

Two of the four helpful peer actions were experienced equally by students with and without physical disabilities: "talked to me at school" and "helped me get away from the situation." However, we found that peers were more likely to spend time with and listen to mistreated students who were not physically disabled (see Table 7.6). Mistreated students with physical disabilities reported experiencing the harmful peer actions of being ignored, made fun of, and blamed more often than students without physical disabilities.

When students with a physical disability came to adults at school about peer mistreatment, adults were more likely to check in with them afterwards

Table 7.6: Prevalence of peer actions toward students with and without a physical disability

	Overall helpfulness score	Prevalence with students with a physical disability	Prevalence with students without a physical disability
Positive peer actions			
Spent time with me, sat with me, or hung out with me	.46	52%	55%
Talked to me at school to encourage me	.44	43%	44%
Helped me get away from the situations where the behavior was going on	.40	38%	38%
Listened to me	.36	58%	64%
Negative peer actions			
Ignored what was going on	−.13	51%	41%
Made fun of me for asking for help or for being treated badly	−.38	30%	19%
Blamed me for what was happening	−.39	31%	20%

and to keep up with increased adult supervision, as compared to mistreated students who did not have a physical disability. However, students with a physical disability also reported a higher rate of all four harmful adult actions (see Table 7.7).

SPECIAL EDUCATION SERVICES

Students receiving special education services reported higher levels of peer mistreatment compared to students in the general population. Like students with a physical disability, boys and girls receiving special education services in all three grade levels also reported higher trauma levels.

Mistreated students who received special education services reported that peers were less likely to spend time with them and listen to them. However, students who received special education help reported that peers were more likely to talk to them at school to encourage them and help them get away from the mistreatment. Students who received help from special education reported higher rates of all three harmful peer actions (see Table 7.8).

Students who received special education services reported higher rates of all four helpful adult actions than students who did not receive special education services. However, students receiving special education services also reported higher rates of all four harmful adult actions (see Table 7.9).

RACE

White students reported disproportionately higher rates of peer mistreatment than students of color. We found that peers were more likely to listen to White students

Table 7.7: Prevalence of adult actions toward students with and without a physical disability

	Overall helpfulness score	Prevalence with students with a physical disability	Prevalence with students without a physical disability
Positive adult actions			
Listened to me	.38	58%	58%
Gave me advice	.34	50%	50%
Checked in with me afterwards to see if the behavior stopped	.31	45%	37%
Kept up increased adult supervision for some time	.13	31%	24%
Negative adult actions			
Ignored what was going on	−.12	43%	30%
Told me that if I acted differently this wouldn't happen to me	−.14	42%	24%
Told me to solve the problem myself	−.17	38%	28%
Told me to stop tattling	−.29	34%	18%

Table 7.8: Prevalence of peer actions toward students who do and do not get help from special education

	Overall helpfulness score	Prevalence with students who get help from special education	Prevalence with students who do not get help from special education
Positive peer actions			
Spent time with me, sat with me, or hung out with me	.46	49%	55%
Talked to me at school to encourage me	.44	47%	43%
Helped me get away from the situations where the behavior was going on	.40	47%	37%
Listened to me	.36	56%	64%
Negative peer actions			
Ignored what was going on	−.13	47%	41%
Made fun of me for asking for help or for being treated badly	−.38	37%	18%
Blamed me for what was happening	−.39	33%	20%

than students of color but were more likely to help students of color get away from situations where the behavior was going on. Students of color reported higher rates of all three harmful peer actions (see Table 7.10).

When students of color came to adults at school about issues related to peer mistreatment, adults were more likely to listen to them and keep up increased supervision

Table 7.9: Prevalence of adult actions toward students who do and do not get help from special education

	Overall helpfulness score	Prevalence with students who get help from special education	Prevalence with students who do not get help from special education
Positive adult actions			
Listened to me	.38	68%	57%
Gave me advice	.34	61%	48%
Checked in with me afterwards to see if the behavior stopped	.31	50%	37%
Kept up increased adult supervision for some time	.13	40%	23%
Negative adult actions			
Ignored what was going on	−.12	41%	29%
Told me that if I acted differently this wouldn't happen to me	−.14	42%	24%
Told me to solve the problem myself	−.17	41%	28%
Told me to stop tattling	−.29	32%	19%

Table 7.10: Prevalence of peer actions toward students of different racial or ethnic backgrounds

	Overall helpfulness score	Prevalence with white students	Prevalence with students of color
Positive peer actions			
Spent time with me, sat with me, or hung out with me	.46	54%	54%
Talked to me at school to encourage me	.44	44%	45%
Helped me get away from the situations where the behavior was going on	.40	37%	40%
Listened to me	.36	66%	60%
Negative peer actions			
Ignored what was going on	−.13	39%	45%
Made fun of me for asking for help or for being treated badly	−.38	17%	24%
Blamed me for what was happening	−.39	19%	24%

over time. Adults at school were also more likely use all four harmful adult actions with students of color (see Table 7.11).

FREE OR REDUCED LUNCH

Socioeconomic status (as measured by eligibility for free or reduced lunch) had no impact on rates of peer mistreatment. Socioeconomic status did impact mistreated students' trauma levels, but only for males. Males who received free or reduced lunch reported higher trauma levels than did their male peers who did not receive free or reduced lunch. As shown in Table 7.12, socioeconomic status did not influence mistreated females' trauma levels.

Students who received or were eligible for free or reduced lunch were more likely to have peers talk to them at school to encourage them and help them get

Table 7.11: Prevalence of adult actions toward students of different racial or ethnic backgrounds

	Overall helpfulness score	Prevalence with white students	Prevalence with students of color
Positive adult actions			
Listened to me	.38	59%	56%
Gave me advice	.34	49%	51%
Checked in with me afterwards to see if the behavior stopped	.31	37%	39%
Kept up increased adult supervision for some time	.13	22%	28%
Negative adult actions			
Ignored what was going on	−.12	27%	35%
Told me that if I acted differently this wouldn't happen to me	−.14	23%	30%
Told me to solve the problem myself	−.17	27%	32%
Told me to stop tattling	−.29	16%	24%

Table 7.12: Student trauma levels by socioeconomic status and gender

	Males	Females
Yes, received free or reduced lunch	M = .82	M = .88
No, did not receive free or reduced lunch	M = .63	M = .85

away from situations where the behavior was going on. Students of lower socioeconomic status were also more likely to be made fun of and blamed by peers for the mistreatment (see Table 7.13).

Students who received or were eligible for free or reduced lunch were more likely to report that adults listened to them, gave them advice, checked in with them afterwards, and kept up increased adult supervision. These students were also more likely to experience all four of the most harmful adult actions (see Table 7.14).

To sum up, our analysis revealed that telling an adult at school was least helpful for students who receive help from special education, are mistreated around issues of sexual orientation, have a physical disability, and receive or are eligible for free or reduced lunch (see Table 7.15).

ENCOURAGING SOCIAL EQUITY

Inequity can be identified and reduced. There are many examples to illustrate this. One of the most successful examples of such an intervention in recent U.S. history is the Title IX program's focus on women in athletics. Title IX increased girls' participation in sports. Title IX used objective measures of equity, paired with the

Table 7.13: Prevalence of peer actions toward students of different socioeconomic backgrounds

	Overall helpfulness score	Prevalence with students who receive or are eligible for free or reduced lunch	Prevalence with students who are not eligible for free or reduced lunch
Positive peer actions			
Spent time with me, sat with me, or hung out with me	.46	55%	54%
Talked to me at school to encourage me	.44	46%	43%
Helped me get away from the situations where the behavior was going on	.40	41%	36%
Listened to me	.36	64%	63%
Negative peer actions			
Ignored what was going on	–.13	43%	41%
Made fun of me for asking for help or for being treated badly	–.38	23%	19%
Blamed me for what was happening	–.39	26%	19%

Table 7.14: Prevalence of adult actions toward students of different socioeconomic backgrounds

	Overall helpfulness score	Prevalence with students who receive or are eligible for free or reduced lunch	Prevalence with students who are not eligible for free or reduced lunch
Positive adult actions			
Listened to me	.38	60%	57%
Gave me advice	.34	53%	48%
Checked in with me afterwards to see if the behavior stopped	.31	42%	36%
Kept up increased adult supervision for some time	.13	27%	24%
Negative adult actions			
Ignored what was going on	−.12	35%	29%
Told me that if I acted differently this wouldn't happen to me	−.14	31%	24%
Told me to solve the problem myself	−.17	32%	28%
Told me to stop tattling	−.29	24%	18%

incentive of receiving or losing federal funding, to require equal spending on and access to sports. It mandated specific measurable changes and included mechanisms to ensure that those changes were made. Equal access and equal funding led to significant changes in outcomes in the form of positive effects on women's education, future employment, and health. It is striking that these outcomes shifted not through awareness building but through concrete change in practices.

Similarly, achieving equity in connection, belonging, and discipline must involve data collection, concrete goals, and accountability for meeting those goals,

Table 7.15: Prevalence and helpfulness of "told an adult at school" about peer mistreatment for different demographic groups

	I didn't do this	Helpfulness score
All mistreated students	70%	.12
Females	71%	.13
White students	72%	.12
Males	69%	.11
Students of color	69%	.10
Receive or are eligible for free or reduced lunch	66%	.02
Students with a physical disability	61%	.01
Students mistreated around issues of sexual orientation	64%	−.05
Students who get help from special education	53%	−.05

rather than just a wish to change attitudes. The outcomes of implementing these steps are likely to be positive and profound. In the following pages, we will describe in detail one school's data-based intervention to demonstrate how anonymous online surveys can guide the work of schools. We will also describe in detail several concrete interventions schools can implement to improve social equity, including reducing the use of biased language and stereotypes and the use of gay-straight alliances. Finally, we will tell one school's story of building feelings of connection for youth who receive help from special education.*

First, however, are some promising interventions, briefly noted:

- Use anonymous student surveys to assess how student subgroups experience school differently.

- Use focus group discussions and other student input to determine systemic issues to be addressed.

- Acknowledge that a range of subgroups exists through open discussion and school posters and other displays. (School displays tell a story, one that students and their families pick up on as they walk the halls.)

- Recruit adults from underconnected subgroups to walk through and observe the school to give feedback based on visuals, practices, and other situations that may be discouraging connection and a sense of belonging.

- Create and support student organizations focused on building connection and alliance.

- Use diversity activities to build empathy and understanding.

- Initiate or strengthen focused silent mentoring, in which educators make an extra effort to greet, show interest in, listen to, and find areas of common interest with youth in underconnected subgroups.

- Initiate or strengthen interest-based activities that are available to all students, which connect adults and youth on the basis of shared interests with others with whom they might not otherwise build relationships.

- Continue to assess connectedness for all students.

Collecting and using data

Collecting anonymous student and staff survey data informs our work to reduce peer mistreatment and improve school climate, enhances buy-in from staff and students, and provides schools with a way to track improvements in a myriad of areas. When interventions are data driven, they can affirm and improve what is working and help the school focus on what needs to change. Without collecting data on an ongoing basis, it is difficult, if not impossible, to know if efforts are leading to improvements for students.

---

*We encourage you to develop and share with us your own successful interventions to make schools welcoming and safe places for all students to learn. You can email Stan Davis at stan@stopbullyingnow.com or Charisse Nixon at cln5@psu.edu.

Many kinds of data can assist in building safe and accepting schools, including disciplinary data, qualitative data gathered from focus groups and discussions, observational data, and quantitative and qualitative data from anonymous surveys. Using data from anonymous online surveys has a number of benefits, including the following:

- Student need not fear peers' or adults' reactions to their statements, and responses can be more authentic.

- Online survey data is easily disaggregated. For example, it can be analyzed by gender, race, age, and special education status, thereby allowing us to understand the experiences of different demographic groups.

- Online surveys can be repeated. This allows tracking of changes over time, permits comparison of schoolwide trends, and enhances the ability to set and follow goals.

- Online surveys can combine quantitative questions with qualitative questions, which allow students to share their ideas and experiences. Students often appreciate being asked about their opinions. Text responses can help schools understand and interpret numerical data accurately.

Both of us facilitate and analyze student and staff surveys for schools. Typically, these surveys are shorter than the Youth Voice Project Survey and include some different questions. To inform an individual school's interventions, it is helpful to gather information in four general areas: school culture, climate, and connection to staff; frequency of specific positive and negative behaviors; attitudes toward both types of behaviors; and adult and peer responses to mistreatment and their impact.

First, we can gauge how students feel about the school environment and their connection to staff and other students by asking questions such as these:

- How many adults at our school do you have a positive relationship with? That means they welcome you to school and you would go to them if you need help.

- Do you feel that you are part of this school?

- Do you feel valued and respected at school?

Second, we can ask about the frequency of specific negative behaviors—such as swearing, cutting in line, exclusion, hitting, and name-calling—based on a variety of factors. Although several problems exist with using frequency data as the primary indicator of the effectiveness of school programs over time, it is helpful to know if youth at school are seeing or hearing negative actions that focus on sexual orientation, disability, social class, race, high academic achievement, or other categories. Asking about a wide range of specific actions gives us a more complete picture than asking only about "bullying." We can ask all youth completing a survey to describe how often they observe different actions while also asking how often youth were the targets of relational or physical aggression.

In Stan's surveys he asks, "In the past month, how often have you seen students do these things at school?" The list of behaviors includes the following:

- Exclusion: Stopping someone from having friends or participating in an activity
- Choosing not to be someone's friend
- Name-calling based on sexual orientation
- Name-calling based on disability
- Name-calling based on race or ethnic/religious background
- Name-calling based on gender
- Name-calling based on family income
- Name-calling based on appearance or body shape
- Name-calling based on ability, either intelligence or athletic
- Pushing, shoving, slapping, or running into other students roughly
- Punching, kicking, or jabbing
- Talking negatively behind someone's back
- Starting or spreading rumors (true or false)
- Indirect use of biased language (that's retarded, that's so gay, etc.)
- Swearing at someone
- Threatening physical harm or violence
- Making faces at people
- Taking things that belong to other students
- Cutting in on other students in line
- Name-calling (jerk, loser, etc.)

Third, we can also ask about young people's attitudes toward the same list of specific negative peer actions. Finding out whether students want adults to take action to stop different behaviors and whether they think peers should tell adults about these behaviors provides useful information in both program planning and in social norms interventions. We can also ask how often youth have seen kind and inclusive behavior.

The last type of question we recommend assesses what adults and youth have done to help youth who are mistreated and how often these actions have helped. It is powerful for youth to hear what students at their school have done to help others. In addition, young people have the opportunity to shape adults' actions by helping them see the importance of acts of support, supervision, and encouragement. We can gather this data by asking questions such as the following:

- What do adults do that helps you feel connected to school?
- What does our school do that helps all students feel safe and belong?
- What else would you like our school to do to help all students feel safe and belong?
- What did other students do that helped you when you were teased, hit, threatened, or excluded? What happened when they did that?

- What did adults at school do that helped you when you were teased, hit, threatened, or excluded? What happened when they did that?

- When other students teased, hit, threatened, or excluded you, did you tell an adult at school? When you told an adult at school, what happened?

The goal of surveys should be to identify areas of strength as well as areas to improve upon. Following a significant analogy we have heard recently, this data should be used as a flashlight rather than a hammer, helping the school see what needs to be done rather than blaming the school for imperfections. If we identify the actions that have led us to success, we can continue and enhance those actions. If we do not identify the actions that have led to success, we are at risk of discontinuing or forgetting to employ those actions.

Reducing the use of biased language and combating gender stereotypes

Language or behavior that limits students' options or teaches bias or prejudice has no place in schools. We believe that these kinds of language and behavior should be discouraged schoolwide, whether or not they are intended as humor.

Students need gentle, daily reminders of how to act, which words to choose, and which words not to choose. We have heard from countless administrators and teachers that by middle school kids should know how to act and how to treat one another. But brain research shows us that during adolescence students may need the most guidance and support with respect to how to act and interact.

The indirect use of biased language is seen in biased statements not directed at any individual, such as "That test is so gay," "That book is so retarded," or "The team played like a bunch of girls." In surveys conducted throughout the United States, Stan has found that indirect biased language is one of the most frequent negative behaviors students observe at school. In almost all middle and high schools, a large majority of students report hearing these comments at least once a week. This observation echoes the results of a school climate survey of gay, lesbian, bisexual, and transgender (GLBT) youth conducted by the Gay Lesbian Straight Education Network (GLSEN, 2009). This study found that 72 percent heard homophobic remarks such as "faggot" or "dyke" frequently or often at school.

Many young people who use biased language do not mean harm by what they say. At the same time, these statements do cause harm. As our friend SuEllen Fried, founder of BullySafe USA and the author of several books, including *Banishing Bullying Behavior* (Fried & Sosland, 2009), reminds us, "Sticks and stones can break your bones, but words can break your heart." The pervasive use of biased language embeds ideas and attitudes in our consciousness. One example is the still too frequent practice of calling boys "girls" to criticize low effort or achievement in sports. We continue to hear from young men that some coaches and other adults in their lives use such statements as motivational tools. It is also true that many coaches and state athletic associations have worked hard to combat this practice, for many good reasons. When young women hear repeated derogatory statements about girls' limitations in athletics, they are less likely to have the confidence to work hard and achieve in those areas of their lives. These statements become self-fulfilling proph-

ONE SCHOOL'S STORY: COLLECTING AND USING DATA

Starrett Junior High School (now Lander Middle School) in Lander, Wyoming, used an anonymous online survey to gather data from all its students. One of the questions the school asked was "How many adults at school do you have a positive relationship with? That means that they welcome you to school and that you would go to them with a small problem."

Analyzing the data obtained by subgroup made it clear that young people in some groups felt less connected to adults. School administrators and the social worker decided to use this data to make positive changes at school.

Over the next school year, they maintained a focus on finding ways to connect with all groups of students. They gathered data again at the end of the next school year. Because these school administrators took responsibility for changing the negative pattern students told them about, they were able to achieve remarkable results (see Table 7.16).

During the period of study, Native American students' reports of feeling safe or safe most of the time at school rose from 50 percent to 76 percent. School staff achieved this improvement through a multistep process. First, as described, educators at this school sought data to evaluate their functioning in connecting with all youth. Second, when they received negative data, they did not make excuses, criticize the way the data were gathered, or seek to "spin" the information. Instead, they acknowledged ownership of the data and worked diligently toward positive change. Third, the administration provided support for remedying this problem at every level, including the school board, the superintendent, and the principal.

They achieved these startling improvements without expensive program add-ons or exceptional resources. We asked staff at the school to identify what they had done to make these changes. Their answers reinforce the idea that we already know how to increase connections with youth and that the most important thing is to raise awareness of the problem and commit to using the good practices that are available to us.

Following is a sampling of staff responses to the question "How did our school increase connections with all youth?"

- Knowing each student's name, greeting students every day, knowing something about their personal lives, going to a sporting event and commenting about their participation

- Having guidance and social worker out at lunch consistently interacting with students

- Focusing on kids who seem to be "loners"

- Consistently being present in the hall every morning in the same spot

- Recognizing accomplishments throughout the school

- Joking with kids and making personal recognitions

- Holding after-school study hall

- Providing individualized help at lunch recess on core classes

- Just being human and nurturing

- Meetings with Native American families to learn ways to build connections

- Hiring great new staff

ecies. As Jackson Katz (1999) illustrates in his film *Tough Guise: Men, Violence and the Crisis in Masculinity,* when young men continually hear the words *girls* or *ladies* used as derogatory terms by people they respect, they are less likely to respect females as children and as adults.

Table 7.16: Prevalence of no positive relationships with adults at school at Starrett Junior High School separated by demographic group

	Prevalence rate of NO positive relationships with adults at school, year 1	Prevalence rate of NO positive relationships with adults at school, year 2
All students	17%	11%
White	13%	11%
Native American	24%	14%
Do not get help from special education	16%	11%
Get help from special education	27%	10%

Note: White and Native American youth were the school's only racial or ethnic groups large enough for meaningful statistical analysis.

We find it remarkable that language that strengthens gender stereotypes is still so widespread. In teachers' rooms, we have heard teachers commiserate with one another when they have a lot of boys in their classes, as though all boys are rowdy and have short attention spans. Stan heard the president of a national association of psychotherapists make the following "joke" at a training presentation: She said that women relieve stress by shopping, whereas men relieve stress by lying on the couch and watching TV.

The effects of gender stereotypes are clear when we ask students what boys are allowed to do and what girls are allowed to do. When we have led such conversations and worked to broaden the list of options for each gender, students come up to us later and say, "Even though I'm a boy, I love to dance, but I don't tell anyone" or "I get called a tomboy because I like to run and play rough."

Research studies have shown that children learn about gender and start to adopt gender related behaviors as early as preschool (Fagot & Leinbach, 1989). For example, children between the ages of two and a half and four are likely to believe that boys are strong and aggressive and that girls are soft and gentle (Powlishta, 2000). Given these strong stereotypes, embedded in our culture from a young age, we need to work very hard to create safe opportunities for both girls and boys to experience their full range of emotions, beliefs, and activities as they continue to develop their unique sense of self.

Adult reactions to hearing biased language, whether direct or indirect, should be based on the potential to do harm instead of on the speaker's intent. We should stop the behavior no matter how it was intended. There is not always time for an extended discussion, but we should not let that lack of time prevent us from reminding young people that biased language stops their classmates from feeling safe and learning—and thus will not be tolerated on any level. When young people see adults intervening consistently to stop the use of biased language, the message is clear that all students are valued members of the school community and have a right to learn.

We can frame these discussions, at least partially, as preparation for meeting job expectations in an adult workplace. This way, whether or not families see acceptance as a positive value, they can understand that youth need to learn to function in workplaces with a diverse group of colleagues. Framing school goals in terms of ensuring that everyone learns provides a core rationale for limiting behavior that interferes with some students' learning. A strong argument can be made that *all* school rules should be based on promoting learning for all. Part of that focus is maintaining a safe, inclusive atmosphere.

It is important, when there is time, to discuss the way in which the indirect use of biased language harms those who hear it. People who are part of the group being denigrated are at risk of learning self-hatred from the incessant barrage of negative stereotypes, metaphors, and statements about that group. This, we believe, is especially true for GLBT youth, who have heard negative statements associated with their sexual orientation for years before they even became aware that they were GLBT. This exposure may lead a person to be preprogrammed for self-hatred from a young age. For those who are not members of the group being denigrated, constant exposure to this language subtly builds and reinforces prejudice at an unconscious level. When we dispute the accuracy of these statements, stop young people and ourselves from using them, and help youth understand the negative effects that can come from exposure to them, we can avoid these negative outcomes.

Small actions of adult support can be meaningful, as the following quotations from the book *Queer Youth Advice for Educators* (Young, 2011) show:

> I had one teacher who specifically stood up for one guy being teased. He said to stop taunting him about being gay, and that it wasn't anything wrong. It's been four years, and I still remember that. It made a world of difference to me to hear someone say that. (p. 14)

> Last week, my TA [teacher's assistant] in my class stood up for me when my history teacher called me a gay and wrote "So Gay" on my paper. All the other kids were laughing at me and I was so upset I left school without permission. But my TA left the class too, she just like stood up and got her purse and left, and she was so upset she was crying. She wrote a letter to the principal saying that the teacher's actions were unacceptable. I would have dropped out if not for her. I love her, she is my hero. (p. 14)

Promoting inclusive, supportive communities

Gay-straight alliances (GSA) combat the frequent isolation of GLBT youth, as well as of other youth who do not fit narrow gender norms. Straight allies at schools with a GSA, both adults and students, show by their involvement that they value GLBT youth. Mark Hatzenbuehler, from Columbia University's Mailman School of Public Health, has reviewed a wide range of data from youth risk behavior surveys conducted in Oregon between 2006 and 2008 (Hatzenbuehler, 2011). Results from his review show that suicide rates are lower for GLBT teens in inclusive school

IMPROVING SOCIAL EQUITY AND CONNECTEDNESS FOR YOUTH WHO GET HELP FROM SPECIAL EDUCATION

In the spring of 2011, Stan worked with a colleague, Chuck Saufler, to survey 3,733 students in 14 schools in Maine under a grant from the Maine Parent Federation, coordinated with the Maine Department of Education. Overall, students who received help from special education in the Maine schools surveyed for this project reported higher rates of physical and relational aggression directed at them than did students who did not get help from special education. Scarborough Middle School, in Scarborough, Maine, was the only school in the survey project where students who received special education services experienced almost the same amount of physical mistreatment and less relational mistreatment as did students who did not get help from special education (see Table 7.17).

Chuck and Stan created an open-ended survey for students and staff at Scarborough Middle School to find out what actions, programs, or other school characteristics may have led to these positive results. The survey used some of the questions from the Youth Voice Project and added some other questions.

Staff members cited the following reasons for their success:

- Commitment to building empathy and inclusion for youth with learning difficulties
- Vigilance in looking for negative actions toward youth receiving special education services
- Efforts to teach young people how to support and include peers with learning issues

They described the work of their health teacher, who had introduced a unit in health class focusing on building students' awareness and empathy around disabilities. One teacher wrote: "Our health curriculum addresses peer respect. This includes how to treat special education kids, with an opportunity to 'walk in their shoes.' This along with the integration and acceptance of them as part of our community, and support for Special Olympics, sends the message that they are just like everyone else."

When students were asked why they thought there was no increase in mistreatment toward youth who receive help from special education at their school, some responded in this way:

- We just make them feel welcome. We treat them like regular students in a regular class.
- I think that the health classes talking about what it's like to have a disability help out a lot. Also, it'd be hard to imagine what it would be like to have a disability, and it makes you feel bad for them. We have also been learning that we should go up to them and get to know them better, or ask them to sit at our lunch table. Because doing this kind of thing could make them feel very happy and welcome in school.
- The adults in our school make sure that special education students get treated fairly by other students.

These students summarize some of the best ways schools can build inclusion: building understanding, establishing a norm of kind and inclusive behavior, helping youth see that kind behavior has positive results, and maintaining adult vigilance to make sure that youth are treated fairly.

communities. Specifically, he found a link between decreased suicide rates and the following three aspects of school climate: GSAs, anti-bullying policies specifically aimed at protecting gay students, and antidiscrimination policies that include sexual orientation.

Table 7.17: Frequency of physical and relational mistreatment twice a month or more often for students who do and do not receive help from special education

	All Maine schools involved (N=3,733)		Scarborough Middle School (N=681)	
	Relational mistreatment	Physical mistreatment	Relational mistreatment	Physical mistreatment
Help from special education	28%	11%	41%	26%
No help from special education	31%	10%	35%	16%

Strikingly, suicide rates were also lower for heterosexual teens in these more inclusive and supportive communities. Hatzenbuehler stated, in a 2011 interview at Columbia University:

This study suggests that we can reduce suicide attempts among [lesbian, gay, and bisexual] youth by improving the social environment and challenging the myth that there is something inherent in being gay that puts gay youth at risk of attempting suicide. Instead, what we've shown is that the social environment strongly influences the prevalence of suicide attempts.

CHAPTER 8

A Tale of Two Schools

We must not, in trying to think about how we can make a big difference, ignore the small daily differences we can make which, over time, add up to big differences that we often cannot foresee.

—Marian Wright Edelman, founder of the Children's Defense Fund

After comparing nearly a million points of data in the Youth Voice Project, we discovered a multitude of associations that were interesting, enigmatic, and occasionally troubling. As discussed earlier, the survey focused on many aspects of peer mistreatment from a sample of 31 schools across the United States. Of these, two schools stood out.

It is natural to compare the extremes of any continuum: the overachievers and those who leave something to be desired. The extremes in the Youth Voice Project data were certainly disparate, with one school seeming to have resolved many of the major problems associated with peer mistreatment and the other having students report peer mistreatment as a major problem of their school climate and culture. The differences are distinct, and we wanted to learn more about what may be driving those differences.

First, we will describe what sets the two schools apart in the data we collected for the Youth Voice Project. We'll call the highest performing school School A and the lowest performing school School F. School A had approximately 600 students. School F had approximately 1,100 students. In terms of actual peer mistreatment, project data revealed that students in School F reported more relational mistreatment than did students in School A. No differences between schools were found in levels of physical mistreatment. Students in School F were more likely to hear others being verbally abused.

Students at School F were more likely to experience cyberbullying, in the form of hurtful texts with sexual content on the Internet and via text message, both in and outside of school. This finding suggests that peer mistreatment of one type is associated with peer mistreatment of other types and, by extension, that lower rates of one type of mistreatment may predict lower rates of other types of mistreatment.

An analysis of the data from all the schools confirmed this theory—showing a very significant relationship between physical and relational mistreatment.

Although frequency of peer mistreatment may represent an important variable to assess, it should not be the only outcome variable. Frequency of peer mistreatment is often the result of many factors, including familial and cultural influences, which are only partly under the school's control. Further, reports of peer mistreatment often increase after young people are sensitized to the issue through educational efforts. Thus, we recommend adding other important outcome variables to any assessment of a school's progress.

We assessed adult responsiveness to peer mistreatment at school by asking what happened when mistreated youth told an adult about their mistreatment. Did things get better? Did things get worse? Did things not change? On average, results indicated that things were more likely to get worse when students told an adult at School F (M = -.06) and things were more likely to get better when students told an adult at School A (M = .21).

We assessed students' feelings of connection to school by asking them to respond to three statements: "I feel like I am part of this school," "I feel valued and respected at school," and "I feel close to adults at my school." Results indicated that students at School A were more likely to feel like they were a part of their school, feel valued and respected at school, and feel close to adults at school, when compared to students at School F (see Table 8.1). The largest difference was in students' feelings of closeness to adults at school.

We also looked at the helpfulness and prevalence of positive and negative adult actions at School A and School F. We found that, in general, adults' actions in School A had more positive outcomes than did adults' actions in School F. For example, when adults kept up with increased supervision in School A, things were likely to get better for mistreated students, whereas they were more likely to get worse for mistreated students in School F. Adults' encouraging mistreated students by giving them advice was also more likely to lead to positive outcomes in School A than in School F. Overall, negative adult actions were more harmful (e.g., "told me to solve the problem myself") and more prevalent for mistreated students in School F than for mistreated students in School A (see Table 8.2).

We also looked at the helpfulness and prevalence of positive and negative peer actions at the two schools to see if youth were picking up on the negative school culture. Unlike adult actions, with the exception of "blamed me for what was hap-

Table 8.1: A comparison of school connection variables for School A and School F

	School A	School F
I feel like I am part of this school	3.93	3.76
I feel valued and respected at school	3.65	3.48
I feel close to adults at my school	3.32	2.98

Note: 1=NO!, 3=Unsure, 5=YES!

Table 8.2: Prevalence and helpfulness of adult actions at School A and School F

	Helpfulness score		Prevalence	
	School A	School F	School A	School F
Positive adult actions				
Listened to me	.36	.32	46%	49%
Gave me advice	.30	.07	39%	42%
Checked in with me afterwards to see if the behavior stopped	.33	.34	32%	31%
Kept up increased adult supervision for some time	.28	−.10	25%	19%
Negative adult actions				
Ignored what was going on	−.08	−.27	22%	29%
Told me that if I acted differently this wouldn't happen to me	−.26	−.25	23%	26%
Told me to solve the problem myself	−.09	−.41	21%	28%
Told me to stop tattling	−.24	−.34	17%	23%

pening," there were very few differences between schools in how peers responded to mistreated students (see Table 8.3).

On reviewing individual text responses from the students at each school, we began to see the differences between schools come into greater focus. Peer mistreatment at School A was, by and large, described as comparatively minor, from complaints that other students "didn't want me at [their] lunch table" to "Someone called me a bad name." This is not to say that these issues shouldn't be addressed, but these issues were in stark contrast to the mistreatment described at School F. In general, descriptions of peer mistreatment at School F were much longer and more disheartening. These descriptions included the following remarks: "i was told i was different because i had diabetes and kids started spreading rumors about me"; "Sometimes people like to trip me, and push past me when we are passing in the

Table 8.3: Prevalence and helpfulness of peer actions at School A and School F

	Helpfulness score		Prevalence	
	School A	School F	School A	School F
Positive peer actions				
Spent time with me, sat with me, or hung out with me	.48	.38	48%	43%
Talked to me at school to encourage me	.44	.52	32%	31%
Helped me get away from the situations where the behavior was going on	.49	.41	28%	29%
Listened to me	.32	.29	46%	49%
Negative peer actions				
Ignored what was going on	−.09	−.22	39%	35%
Made fun of me for asking for help or for being treated badly	−.54	−.55	14%	15%
Blamed me for what was happening	−.50	−.37	14%	20%

hall. I don't think they co[n]sider other peoples feelings"; and "In 5 grade I got put down every day and called names. I was in sixth grade when I had rumors at me because they say I was w[e]ird and gay."

When students were asked what they wished teachers would have done to help, some responses from School F were downright distressing. From the saddening, but slightly more mild "[I] wish they [would've] told the whole school to leave me alone" all the way to "I wish they would've help me kill them," the answers certainly reflected a school in serious trouble. Some students wished teachers would have done "more anti-bullying stuff" or even "actually helped me."

These responses are in direct contrast to the responses of students at School A, who said they wished school staff would have "gave pun[i]shments . . . only little ones though" and "I think they did all I really wanted them to do." There were students who were unhappy with their teachers' response to the situation, but there were no comments about killing their classmates or anything even remotely close.

Upon initial inspection, the schools seemed to be relatively similar. They were both public middle schools (one grades 6–8, the other grades 4–8), with a diverse portrait of students and a White majority. One school spent around $9,000 per student per year, and the other spent around $10,000 per student, most of which was on instructional expenses. Students at both schools had test scores that were slightly above their state average and comparatively similar. Perhaps, then, the distinction between the two schools lies not in demographics and financial expenditures but on something less tangible.

The discrepancy could be first observed by viewing the activities each school offered. School A offered its students a total of 15 varsity sports. School F offered 7. School A offered 29 clubs, whereas School F offered 11. This disparity is especially striking when we remember that School A had slightly more than half as many students as School F.

The mission statements of the two schools also revealed substantial differences. School F's mission statement read more like boilerplate than an actual statement of goals. It referred vaguely to "maintaining excellence" at the school. School A broke its mission down into specific components. It precisely defined each component and reported how it was measured and maintained within the school. The mission statement included items such as the "personalization of learning experiences" to a commitment to "fostering a love of lifelong learning." These statements reflected the great deal of thought that went into the shaping of School A's educational goals. In short, School A identified important and measureable outcomes and developed a system to meet them.

An interview with members of School A's administration netted an in-depth description of the school's advisor-advisee program. Some advisor-advisee programs in other schools, administrators said, can be places where students "get nagged about their homework or where forms get filled out." By contrast, School A expanded its pool of potential advisors by bringing in mentors from across the building, such as gym teachers who did not have a homeroom of their own, and focused advisor-advisee times on building mentoring connections. In contrast, School F did not have any mentoring or advisor-advisee programs described in its literature. Thus, it is possible that the connections gained through a network of mentors and mentees contributed to the success of School A.

We can draw some preliminary conclusions from looking at our brief analysis of these two schools. The data suggest that schools working to create safer, more supportive school climates need to look beyond their static, demographic variables to more dynamic, relational variables. We are often quick to explain school outcomes with static variables such as available school resources, student test scores, or socioeconomic status. Although this approach may be tempting, our data suggest that this is not the whole story. Instead, we need to look at variables supporting (or not supporting) positive relationships within the school culture.

When taken together, these findings suggest that schools aiming to reduce the frequency and negative impact of peer mistreatment should work to create a climate conducive not just to learning but also to tolerance, kindness, and the building of positive social connections among peers of many different groups. These qualities should be reflected in everything from the school's mission statement to values espoused by the teachers to the way classes are conducted. Programs that have the potential to build positive social alliances among students who would not normally interact are of paramount importance.

Our analysis of the two schools suggests that meaningful connections among students and between students and staff are important factors contributing to the success of supportive schools. School A encouraged meaningful connections through a variety of clubs and activities and the advisor-advisee program. Differences were found in how the two schools developed and defined their mission statements. School F chose a more top-down model, whereas School A adopted a more inclusive, bottom-up approach. School A also engaged both students and staff in establishing and maintaining the school's code of ethics.

We wanted to learn as much as possible about the highest performing school in the hope of identifying those characteristics that contributed to positive school functioning. We also wanted to find out what the school culture was like and how students and staff interacted. Ideally, if we could better understand those factors that significantly contributed to a positive school climate, we could then help other schools act accordingly.

Brunswick Junior High School in Brunswick, Maine, was School A. In order to learn more about this school's high performance, Stan interviewed staff and students there. He audiorecorded all his discussions, and students at Penn State, The Behrend College, transcribed and summarized these recorded discussions.* To begin the interviews, Stan brought the positive survey results to the school and asked staff and students how the school had achieved the results. Two major themes emerged from the interviews: connection and code of ethics. Intentional connections were promoted within the day-to-day lives of students at Brunswick Junior High School through three programs: peer partners, an advisor-advisee program, and after-school programming. A consistent districtwide code of ethics created and reinforced a culture of helpfulness.

---

*We want to thank two students especially for their work on this analysis: Carl Kallgren IV and Denise Hillen.

PEER PARTNERS

The peer partners program appeared to operate as a mentoring effort focused on helping incoming sixth graders transition successfully to the school. This is how students described the peer partners program:

> "Peer partners are groups of six or seven with all the grades combined. It makes it easier to talk to people around our age in sixth, seventh and eighth grade . . . not just a teacher."

> "It's just like this program where . . . there are eighth graders, you sign up to be peer partners and you have a group of six or seven kids and you really just like get to know them. So then instead of just all the eighth graders know each other it's kind of like . . . you really get to know everybody down in the sixth grade. The eighth graders really don't get to see the sixth graders that much and get to know them. So this is a way to help them with the new transformation from the elementary school to the junior high and what's different."

> "It's a way if a sixth grader has a problem with something in the school either from when they were transferring from the elementary school to the junior high . . . or any other time to talk to someone more close to their age or someone more comfortable that they are expressing their feelings with or problems instead of a teacher and we can either go to a teacher and tell them if it's serious or try to help them work though it themselves."

> "Because like for me, I know for me it's always easier to talk to someone who is your age rather than a teacher. I mean I can talk to a teacher but I feel more comfortable talking to someone my age."

This is how one staff member described the peer partners program:

> "I'm a sixth-grade advisor and I know that my advisees find it very cool that they can walk down the hall and greet an eighth grader by name and be greeted by name by an eighth grader, kind of the role models of the school, so I think it's been really effective for them too. . . . They get kind of excited about it."

Here is a comment from a student who transferred into Brunswick Junior High School and who previously attended a school where they did not have peer partners:

> "I was just gonna say I'm not a part of peer partners or anything but I remember in sixth grade coming into a school where they didn't have peer partners . . . but if you had a problem that you weren't sure with or you didn't have someone to go to now I realize like a lot of sixth graders now. They have someone to like turn to and if there's stuff . . . they can always have someone to ask."

ADVISOR-ADVISEE PROGRAM

The advisor-advisee program included a separate time during the school day when small groups of students and adults had fun together. Several students and teachers commented about the value of the small group size. Students were also quick to comment about how fun the advisor-advisee times were:

> "It's better to have small groups, so we can really get to know the other kids . . . and the teachers really connect with you."

> "Every six weeks or so, there's this extra time where they have a whole period at the end of the day and they do really neat stuff; they make crazy costumes out of newspapers and they play, and they just do really fun stuff."

Supportive administration seems to be an integral part of the advisor-advisee program:

> "Rather than having teachers beg the administration to do some sort of program to help the kids, it is the administration themselves that are pushing for this, which would lead to its success, and to an atmosphere that is conducive to positive, fun, creative time for the students."

Adult advisors included gym teachers, art teachers, and other staff in addition to academic teachers. This expanded the pool of advisors and increased the number of adults at school with whom students can interact and form potential meaningful connections. This advisor-advisee time encouraged meaningful relationships between adults and students at school. As one student noted:

> "I feel like the teachers make an effort to become friends with you, not just be a teacher. [They] make you feel at home, for example . . . like you have a job and you're important."

AFTER-SCHOOL PROGRAMS

Students also identified after-school programs as supportive opportunities for students to connect with one another. In their comments, several students stressed that the activities included more than athletics:

> "After-school groups help a lot. Sixth, seventh, and eighth graders can all join in, so you get to know a lot more people."

> "The school is good about how many activities there are. Everyone can feel like they are part of something, even if they might not be into sports. They might be into debate team . . . and stuff like that, so there's kind of something for everyone."

CODE OF ETHICS

Another theme that emerged from the interviews at School A was a consistent districtwide code of ethics that created a culture of helpfulness. Students were taught about the code in elementary school, and it was continued and reinforced in middle and high school. Staff described the code of ethics in the following ways:

- Honesty, courage and responsibility.
- More compassion, respect and fairness.

- Use simple manners; don't say "shut-up," say "please."

The code of ethics is an ongoing work based on student involvement and leadership. The school celebrates success on a regular basis. One staff member gave this description:

"At the end of the program we have 15 minutes where everyone kind of celebrates successes and the students nominate each other for small actions through the afternoon that they noticed, and it's really neat because a lot of time the staff will nominate students, but I've noticed that over time, students are very serious and they'll come up to me in the middle of program and be like I need a good news report card I just saw this, and they really don't necessarily need to be personal friends. They're appreciating the structure in the guidelines that are set clearly and upheld, and it creates a safe environment, and they are the ones that are making sure that it is promoted through the program. It's really neat to see the students take that leadership role."

This code of ethics just described is in sharp contrast to School F's code, in which the words *respect, code of conduct*, and other terms are used in a top-down manner, with adults defining expected behavior without collaborating with students. Getting students involved in creating the code and recognizing students who are doing a good job is clearly meaningful for students.

Another important aspect of the code of ethics at Brunswick Junior High School is a consistent adult response. Students commented that when they report a problem to staff, adults act right away:

"Teachers are fast responders and don't let things escalate."

"You can count on them. They pay attention."

To encourage students to uphold the code of ethics, school staff give out coupons to reinforce positive student behavior such as respect, compassion, fairness, or taking responsibility. This is one example of positive reinforcement, which seems to be prevalent throughout the school and helps encourage students continue to engage in prosocial behavior.

CHAPTER 9

Summary and Recommendations

We have both been active in the modern bullying prevention movement from its beginning, and we build on work that has been done by a wide range of researchers and practitioners, including Dan Olweus and his colleagues in the Olweus Bullying Prevention Program; Dorothea Ross; the Committee for Children, creators of the Second Step program; Susan Limber and her colleagues at the Institute on Family and Neighborhood Life; the late Nicki Crick and her colleagues at the Institute of Child Development; Sameer Hinduja and Justin Patchin at the Cyberbullying Research Center; and many others.

On the basis of our work with schools and the research described in this book, we propose a new paradigm for bullying prevention that builds on the efforts of many in this field and on other research in social psychology, criminological research, and research in developmental and educational psychology. We continue the emphasis of these earlier researchers on interventions that aim to examine and improve the climate and culture of schools as communities, rather than those that focus only on the behavior of individuals. We agree with our colleagues that this undertaking requires significant effort and time and that one talk to children by a visiting expert, theater troupe, or workshop (no matter how well-crafted) is unlikely to cause lasting change. Instead, change must come from the day-to-day efforts of teachers, counselors, administrators, and parents in the school community, as well as from the involvement of a majority of students.

WHAT DOESN'T WORK

Donald Schon, in his 1983 book, *The Reflective Practitioner: How Professionals Think in Action,* presents clearly the crucial idea that we can claim to be professionals only if we continually evaluate the actions and interventions we use. He stresses the need for clear outcome goals and for ongoing conscious reflection about whether the interventions we are using are actually reaching the goals we have set. The other choice, Schon explains, is for us to continue to use the techniques that we have been taught with no regard for whether they are reaching our goals.

In the spirit of Schon's work, we have looked at the bullying prevention field and have come to believe that three practices are actually doing more harm than

139

good. First, we see significant evidence from our experience and research that the common practice of teaching youth the difference between "tattling" and "telling" has long-lasting negative results. In our research, mistreated youth told us that adults often told them to "stop tattling" when they asked those adults for help. Youth told us that this was the adult action most likely to lead to negative outcomes. We have both experienced many situations in which students avoided telling adults the truth about what had been done to them or to others because they didn't want to be "tattletales." As we have discussed, we believe it is time to abandon the idea that it is ever wrong for youth to express honest concerns to adults. That does not mean that adults have to solve every problem for young people. It does mean that we should stop teaching youth not to tell us about their problems.

Second, our research and professional experience over the past decades convinces us that it is time to abandon the idea that mistreated youth have somehow caused their mistreatment by their lack of assertion or annoying behavior. Linked to this idea is the commonly expressed belief that if mistreated youth would only speak up, not let the mistreater know they are bothered by negative actions, or walk away, the mistreatment would stop. As we have shown, these actions are often not helpful for mistreated youth, and this advice can lead youth to blame themselves for what has been done to them and thus to accept the negative opinions of their tormentors.

Third, we have come to believe that widespread use of the limited concept of bullying has had significant unintended negative effects. Adults and youth have been taught to distinguish between bullying—usually defined as including the intent to harm, a power differential, and repetition—and other peer mistreatment. In our work with youth and educators in the United States and around the world, we have heard numerous accounts of harmful peer actions that were ignored because the adult observing them "knew that kid didn't mean any harm." We have heard young people describe their own hurtful actions as acceptable because they are sure that they are not "bullies" or that they didn't mean to do harm. Harm can be done even if there is no intent to harm. Harm can be done when there is no power differential. Harm can be done by the actions of a close friend. Harm can be done by one event.

We believe that in deciding what to do about students' behavior, school staff should look at the potential for harm rather than at our subjective and fallible judgment of whether harm is intended or whether the person calling names has more social status than the target. The use of the term *bullying* encourages many people to look for "bullies" rather than to look at the actions that anyone may choose and that can do harm no matter who uses them. In brief, we should talk about what an individual does, not who the person is.

WHAT DOES WORK

We have presented a wide range of research, including our own, in this book. We have discussed many strategies that have been used successfully. In this section we will give an overview of the "big ideas" in the book in the effort to help you organize and use the information in meaningful ways to optimize students' development and reduce peer mistreatment. There are four unifying themes to our recommendations. We call these themes the "Four Rs": respect, relationships, resiliency, and responsiveness.

Respect

When a school works to build clear definitions of respectful behavior with meaningful student involvement, most students will uphold and follow those behavioral standards. Students at Brunswick Junior High School in Brunswick, Maine, told us how much they valued being in a school where they were involved in helping to write the code of ethics. Schools with responsive classrooms benefit from having students define which classroom actions will help them learn and grow and which actions will not. We have heard from teachers all over the world that students are more likely to follow behavior standards that they help to design.

When educators follow up with student designed behavioral expectations by responding effectively and consistently when those standards are not followed, they show their care and concern. When educators follow up by helping students observe the effects of their own positive behaviors, they help young people internalize the reasons for their positive actions.

When we see kind, inclusive, cooperative behavior, we have four possible reactions: we can ignore the behavior, tell students how we feel about what they have done, use tangible rewards, or help youth see the positive outcomes of their own actions. When we ignore positive behaviors, we lose a valuable teaching opportunity.

When we tell students how we feel about what they have done, we can increase positive behavior in the short term in the lower grades. However, teaching students that they should act in kind, cooperative ways to make adults happy can have unintended negative outcomes as students enter adolescence and no longer wish to please adults.

Similarly, when we use tangible rewards, such as extra recess time, to encourage kind actions, we may be able to increase the frequency of kind behavior in the short run. However, decades of research studies have documented that extrinsic rewards interfere with the development of internal motivation. (See Deci & Flaste, 1996, for an authoritative presentation of the long-term negative influences of tangible rewards on intrinsic motivation.)

The fourth and most effective reaction is to help youth observe their own positive actions and recognize the subsequent positive outcomes of those actions. We can do this by asking questions such as "When this week did we work especially well together?" and "During that time, what did students do to make our classroom a good place for learning?" The most crucial question is "What happened next when people did those things?" As educators, our goal is to develop young people's intrinsic motivation to continue kind, respectful behavior. We can help young people develop enduring intrinsic motivation when we help them see the real and positive outcomes of specific respectful actions. Frequent discussion of respectful actions and their outcomes is likely to contribute to transforming a code of ethics from a piece of paper to a core element of school climate. A clear schoolwide definition of respectful behavior toward peers, consistently enforced on a daily basis, significantly contributes to the health of the school community.

Relationships

As noted in chapter 3, belonging is a fundamental human need (Baumeister & Leary, 1995). The American psychologist Abraham Maslow (1943, 1954), well-known for his hierarchy of needs theory, also considers belonging a basic need, second only to survival and safety. In a recent review of the relationship between social connection and physical health, Holt-Lunstad and Smith (2012) conclude that "reducing mortality risk via social factors represents a major opportunity and challenge for the improvement of health care" (p. 51).

The Youth Voice Project research confirms the work of many others in demonstrating that being part of school and receiving peer and adult support reduces the trauma of peer mistreatment. We have presented a range of strategies for assessing connectedness, for addressing inequities in connection, and for building relationships among students and between students and educators. What follows is a summary of the most promising strategies we can use to build connection:

- We can start by using survey data to identify inequities in rates of mistreatment and school connectedness.

- When we find inequities, we can address them and continue to assess our performance. The example of Lander Middle School in Lander, Wyoming, shows us that caring adults can improve connections with diverse subgroups without expensive initiatives.

- We can build and protect activities that connect students with one another and with school staff. Adviser-advisee times, class meetings, interest-based activities, and meaningful service projects are all likely to increase connectedness.

- We can build connections for disconnected and mistreated youth through mentoring initiatives that involve both staff and students in purposefully reaching out to marginalized youth.

- Perhaps most important, adults at school can express unconditional positive regard to all students. As we strengthen the web of positive connections that includes all members of the school community, we build ties that help everyone learn and thrive.

Resiliency

Many decades of research have documented resiliency as an important determinant of life outcomes. We have identified five key elements that build students' resiliency:

- First, we can create a web of positive connections makes everyone stronger and therefore less likely to be harmed if they are mistreated by peers.

- Second, we can follow Myrna Shure's research (Shure, 2000, 2001a, 2001b) and teach all youth the cognitive skills of social problem solving so they can try different solutions instead of giving up when they experience failure. Using a lack of success in social problem solving as a sign to consider backup plans can help youth avoid feelings of helplessness.

- Third, we can help youth develop what Carol Dweck (2006) calls "growth mindsets" so they see their successes as the result of choices and actions they have made in addition to the support they have received from others. When we support growth mindset thinking, youth can respond to failure or mistreatment or frustration without helplessness. They can seek and use support.

- Fourth, we can teach and support youth in filtering out others' negative statements about them. When we do this, we empower young people to choose how they feel about themselves. With the help of supportive peer and adult encouragement, students can choose not to let other students' negative behaviors have power over them.

- Fifth, we can involve youth in activities that strengthen them. Hobbies and other mastery activities help young people experience the strength that comes from earned achievement. Perhaps most important, meaningful service to others helps young people build durable self-esteem, self-efficacy, and habits of helping and caring. Schools can be a positive force in building resiliency and subsequently may have a powerful impact on students' lifelong development.

Responsiveness

We help reduce peer mistreatment and help youth who have been mistreated when we respond effectively. There are four elements in that response:

- First, when adults act consistently in the moment to interrupt and discourage hurtful speech and actions, they show youth that they care. Consistent adult responses to enforce schoolwide behavior standards help youth choose kind, inclusive behaviors instead of potentially hurtful ones.

- Second, when we show mistreated youth that we care about them and that we do not agree with those who might criticize or demean them, we shield them from the harm that can come from that criticism. The youth in our study identified "listened to me" as the most helpful adult action in response to peer mistreatment.

- Third, when we maintain supervision over time and check back with mistreated youth to see if things have gotten better, we are more able to protect youth from repeated mistreatment.

- Fourth, we can encourage students' peers to include, support, and encourage mistreated youth. In doing so, we will be promoting the one intervention that youth in our research reported helped them the most: being included by their peers. We can make this essential positive peer support more likely when we abandon the well-meaning advice that caring peers should confront those who mistreat. Instead, we propose a safer and more effective focus for peer action: inclusion and emotional support.

When we respond to mistreatment through a mix of supervision, effective consequences, and steps to increase connection and support, we are most likely to make things better. Within all four of these interventions, we help reduce peer mistreatment and optimize student outcomes when we consider individual students' unique developmental needs and challenges.

CONCLUSIONS

While we were designing the Youth Voice Project Survey, a colleague asked us about the wording of one of the questions. She asked whether we meant to ask youth if any particular action led to things getting better, led to no change, or led to things getting worse. Wouldn't we be better off, she asked, if we asked whether each action stopped the bullying or increased the bullying? We talked this important question over with her and with other colleagues. It became clear to us in these discussions that we were eager to know how youth defined "things getting better," so we kept the open-ended wording we had first written. We are very glad that we made this seemingly insignificant decision. We have learned through analyzing the numerical data and through reading thousands of text responses that many youth said that things got better for them as a result of actions that did nothing to stop the mistreatment. Young people benefited from private expressions of support and reassurance from adults and peers. Youth benefited from thinking about what had been done to them in different ways. Youth told us they benefited from prayer and from involvement in activities they love. And, of course, youth told us that they benefited from adult actions that stopped the mistreatment.

We hope that our research leads to an increased focus on building resiliency and social support for youth. These strategies can and should be applied preventively, to build strength in all youth in case they are mistreated. These strategies should also be extended to youth who have been mistreated.

We propose a number of future directions for research that asks youth to define helpful strategies in the face of mistreatment:

- First, we would like to learn more about of the needs and experiences of subgroups of youth we did not focus on, including gifted and talented youth, whom we know are more likely than other students to find some schools a hostile place.

- Second, we would like more exploration of the different types and results of humor in the face of mistreatment.

- Third, we would like to learn more about the protective mechanisms youth told about in text responses that had not been in our questionnaire, including prayer, membership in both religious and secular youth groups, and service to others. We would also like to learn more about the effectiveness of voluntary forgiveness in reducing students' trauma levels following peer mistreatment.

- Fourth, we would like to see more study of what elements of school procedure and climate lead to increases in the numbers of youth who say that things got better when they told an adult at school about mistreatment.

- Fifth, we would like to learn more about ways adults at the high school level can improve student-adult connections and the outcome of students' asking adults for help.

One last statement before the end of this book: Both of us travel quite a bit in our work, and in airports we have often seen an older person with a military background approach a young service member in uniform to thank the person for his or her service to our country. We want to take this moment to say something similar to teachers, counselors, principals, school secretaries, bus drivers, tutors, and all the other adults who make the welfare of young people their life's work. Thank you for your service to our country. Thank you for building a bright future for our nation and our world by educating, supporting, and encouraging tomorrow's adults. Educators' work is often difficult and thankless. It seems to us, though, that few people do work that is more important. Thank you for your service.

APPENDIX

Youth Voice Project Survey

What is this project about?* You are being asked to be part of a research study. Studies like this one will help adults find out what works best to reduce bullying in the school setting. This form will tell you about the study to help you decide whether or not you want to participate. You can ask any questions you have before making up your mind. It is okay to say "No" if you don't want to be in the study. If you say "Yes" you can change your mind and quit being in the study at any time without getting in trouble. An adult (parent or guardian) has said it's okay for you to be in the study.

What is the research about? This project will help educators find out what works the best to reduce bullying in your school. We believe it is time for young people like you to help tell us what might be done to stop the bullying. We believe that you know a lot about how we can begin to make this better for other kids.

How long will it take me? The survey lasts about 40–45 minutes (but could be shorter). If you feel uncomfortable answering any of the questions, you can skip those questions.

Voluntary participation: Your class grade will not be affected if you participate or decide that you do not want to participate. When we get the results back from the study, we would be happy to share them with your class. It feels good to be involved in a project to help make things better in your school.

Confidentiality of answers: All of the answers you choose on the survey will remain confidential, which means that it will be kept a secret between you and the researchers only. The researchers will analyze the data, but never match your answers with your name or other information about you when they summarize, present, or publish the results of the research. You can trust that we will not share your individual answers with anyone.

If you do not want to participate in the research, please tell your teacher so that she/he makes sure to remove your answers from the survey.

---

*These pages include the Youth Voice Project Survey in its entirety. Please email Charisse Nixon at cln5@psu.edu for permission to use any or all questions.

1. Please indicate your consent to participate in this research by checking the appropriate box below. I understand the above information and have had all of my questions about participation in this research project answered.

    ◯ Yes, I voluntarily agree to participate in this survey.

    ◯ No, I do not wish to participate in this survey.

2. Are you male or female?

    ◯ Male

    ◯ Female

    ◯ Prefer not to answer

3. What grade are you in?

    ◯ 5

    ◯ 6

    ◯ 7

    ◯ 8

    ◯ 9

    ◯ 10

    ◯ 11

    ◯ 12

4. How old are you?

    ◯ 11 or younger

    ◯ 12

    ◯ 13

    ◯ 14

    ◯ 15

    ◯ 16

    ◯ 17

    ◯ 18

    ◯ 19 or older

5. Do you have any type of physical disability?

    ◯ Yes

❍ No

6. Do you receive any help from special education?

❍ Yes

❍ No

7. How would you describe your racial or cultural background?

❍ Native American

❍ African American

❍ Hispanic American

❍ Native Hawaiian

❍ Pacific Islander

❍ White

❍ Asian American

❍ Multiracial

❍ Other

❍ Prefer not to answer

8. Do you get reduced or free hot lunches at school, or are you eligible for free or reduced lunch?

❍ Yes

❍ No

9. Are you currently living with:

❍ Two birth parents

❍ One birth parent (you may also live with other adults)

❍ Neither birth parent

10. Have your parents immigrated to the United States within the past 2 years?

❍ Yes

❍ No

11. I feel like I am part of this school.

❍ NO!

❍ No

❍ Unsure

○ Yes

○ YES!

12. I feel valued and respected at school.

　○ NO!

　○ No

　○ Unsure

　○ Yes

　○ YES!

13. I feel close to adults at my school.

　○ NO!

　○ No

　○ Unsure

　○ Yes

　○ YES!

14. In the past month, how often have students at your school hurt you emotionally or excluded you?

　○ Every day

　○ Once a week

　○ Two or three times a month

　○ One time

　○ Never

15. In the past month, how often have students at your school threatened to hurt you or hurt you physically?

　○ Every day

　○ Once a week

　○ Two or three times a month

　○ One time

　○ Never

16. In the past month at school, how often did you see or hear name-calling or threatening comments that could hurt someone's feelings or make them feel unsafe?

　○ Every day

○ Once a week

○ Two or three times a month

○ One time

○ Never

17. When you heard name-calling or threats that could hurt someone's feelings or make them feel unsafe, what did you do? What happened when you did that? Please click one option for each action.

	I didn't do this	I did this and things got worse	I did this and things didn't change	I did this and things got better
I angrily told the person who was calling names to stop it!	○	○	○	○
Listened to the target(s).	○	○	○	○
I kindly asked the person who was calling names to stop.	○	○	○	○
I ignored what was going on or watched quietly.	○	○	○	○
I spent time with the target(s), sat with them, or hung out with them.	○	○	○	○
I gave the target(s) advice about what they should do.	○	○	○	○
I blamed the target(s) for what was happening.	○	○	○	○
I made fun of the target(s) for asking for help or for being treated badly.	○	○	○	○
I called or emailed or texted or IM'd the target(s) to encourage them.	○	○	○	○
I talked to the target(s) at school to encourage them.	○	○	○	○
I told an adult at school.	○	○	○	○
I told an adult at home.	○	○	○	○
I helped the target(s) to tell an adult.	○	○	○	○
I helped the target(s) get away from situations where the behavior was going on.	○	○	○	○

	I didn't do this	I did this and things got worse	I did this and things didn't change	I did this and things got better
I distracted the people who were calling names or threatening others.	○	○	○	○

Other (What else did you do and how much did it help?)

18. In the past month at school, how often did you see hitting, kicking, or other acts of physical aggression that could hurt someone?

○ Every day

○ Once a week

○ Two or three times a month

○ One time

○ Never

19. When you saw hitting, kicking, or other physically aggressive acts that could hurt someone, what did you do? What happened when you did that? Please click one option for each action.

	I didn't do this	I did this and things got worse	I did this and things didn't change	I did this and things got better
I angrily told the person who was calling names to stop it!	○	○	○	○
Listened to the target(s).	○	○	○	○
I kindly asked the person who was calling names to stop.	○	○	○	○
I ignored what was going on or watched quietly.	○	○	○	○
I spent time with the target(s), sat with them, or hung out with them.	○	○	○	○
I gave the target(s) advice about what they should do.	○	○	○	○
I blamed the target(s) for what was happening.	○	○	○	○
I made fun of the target(s) for asking for help or for being treated badly.	○	○	○	○
I called or emailed or texted or IM'd the target(s) to encourage them.	○	○	○	○
I talked to the target(s) at school to encourage them.	○	○	○	○

I told an adult at school.	○	○	○	○
I told an adult at home.	○	○	○	○
I helped the target(s) to tell an adult.	○	○	○	○
I helped the target(s) get away from situations where the behavior was going on.	○	○	○	○
I distracted the people who were calling names or threatening others.	○	○	○	○
Other (What else did you do and how much did it help?)				

20. In the past month at school, how often did you see or hear rumor spreading, exclusion, or students working together to be mean to someone?

    ○ Every day

    ○ Once a week

    ○ Two or three times a month

    ○ One time

    ○ Never

21. When you saw or heard rumor spreading, exclusion, or students working together to be mean to someone, what did you do? What happened when you did that? Please click one option for each action.

	I didn't do this	I did this and things got worse	I did this and things didn't change	I did this and things got better
I angrily told the person who was calling names to stop it!	○	○	○	○
Listened to the target(s).	○	○	○	○
I kindly asked the person who was calling names to stop.	○	○	○	○
I ignored what was going on or watched quietly.	○	○	○	○
I spent time with the target(s), sat with them, or hung out with them.	○	○	○	○
I gave the target(s) advice about what they should do.	○	○	○	○
I blamed the target(s) for what was happening.	○	○	○	○

	I didn't do this	I did this and things got worse	I did this and things didn't change	I did this and things got better
I made fun of the target(s) for asking for help or for being treated badly.	◯	◯	◯	◯
I called or emailed or texted or IM'd the target(s) to encourage them.	◯	◯	◯	◯
I talked to the target(s) at school to encourage them.	◯	◯	◯	◯
I told an adult at school.	◯	◯	◯	◯
I told an adult at home.	◯	◯	◯	◯
I helped the target(s) to tell an adult.	◯	◯	◯	◯
I helped the target(s) get away from situations where the behavior was going on.	◯	◯	◯	◯
I distracted the people who were calling names or threatening others.	◯	◯	◯	◯

Other (What else did you do and how much did it help?)

22. In the past month at school, how often did you see harassment based on sexual orientation, religion, race, or gender?

    ◯ Every day

    ◯ Once a week

    ◯ Two or three times a month

    ◯ One time

    ◯ Never

23. When you saw harassment based on race, gender, religion or sexual orientation, what did you do? What happened when you did that? Please click one option for each action.

	I didn't do this	I did this and things got worse	I did this and things didn't change	I did this and things got better
I angrily told the person who was calling names to stop it!	◯	◯	◯	◯
Listened to the target(s).	◯	◯	◯	◯
I kindly asked the person who was calling names to stop.	◯	◯	◯	◯

I ignored what was going on or watched quietly.	O	O	O	O
I spent time with the target(s), sat with them, or hung out with them.	O	O	O	O
I gave the target(s) advice about what they should do.	O	O	O	O
I blamed the target(s) for what was happening.	O	O	O	O
I made fun of the target(s) for asking for help or for being treated badly.	O	O	O	O
I called or emailed or texted or IM'd the target(s) to encourage them.	O	O	O	O
I talked to the target(s) at school to encourage them.	O	O	O	O
I told an adult at school.	O	O	O	O
I told an adult at home.	O	O	O	O
I helped the target(s) to tell an adult.	O	O	O	O
I helped the target(s) get away from situations where the behavior was going on.	O	O	O	O
I distracted the people who were calling names or threatening others.	O	O	O	O
Other (What else did you do and how much did it help?)				

24. Which of these things happened to you? You may click more than one option.

   O I was called names.

   O Rumors were spread about me.

   O I was excluded or students worked together to be mean to me.

   O I was threatened.

   O I was hit, kicked, or otherwise physically hurt.

   O Other (please specify)

25. Who called you names at school that hurt you? You may click more than one option.

   O Male students

○ Female students

○ Teachers or other school staff

26. Did the people who hurt you focus on any of these issues? You may click more than one option. Please do not include any names.

    ○ Race

    ○ Looks

    ○ Gender or gender expression

    ○ Sexual orientation

    ○ Religion

    ○ Family income

    ○ Body shape

    ○ Disability

    ○ Other (please specify)

27. Who spread rumors about you or excluded you to hurt your feelings? You may check one or more answers.

    ○ Male students at school

    ○ Female students at school

    ○ Teachers or other adults at school

28. Who hit, pushed, or threatened you at school? You may check one or more answers.

    ○ Male students at school

    ○ Female students at school

    ○ Teachers or other adults at school

29. If you feel comfortable, please describe what happened to you. Because this is an confidential survey, please also tell an adult you trust at school about what happened if you have not already done that. Please do not include any names.

30. Where did these things happen? You may click more than one choice.

    ○ In the cafeteria

    ○ In the classroom

    ○ In the hallways

    ○ In the restrooms

○ On the Internet when I was at school

○ On the Internet when I was out of school

○ On the school bus

○ Outside of school

○ Sports

○ Using text messaging when I was at school

○ Using text messaging when I was out of school

○ Walking to or from school

○ Other (please specify)

31. How severe was the impact of what they did on you?

○ Mild: What they did bothered me only a little.

○ Moderate: It bothered me quite a bit.

○ Severe: I had or have trouble eating, sleeping, or enjoying myself because of what happened to me.

○ Very severe: I felt or feel unsafe and threatened because of what happened to me.

32. Did you do any of these things about what was done to you? What helped? Please click one option for each action.

	I didn't do this	I did it and things got worse	I did it and nothing changed	I did it and things got better
Pretended it didn't bother me.	○	○	○	○
Reminded myself that what they are doing is not my fault and that THEY are the ones who are doing something wrong.	○	○	○	○
Made plans to get back at them or fight them.	○	○	○	○
Hit them or fought them.	○	○	○	○
Told the person or people to stop.	○	○	○	○
Did nothing.	○	○	○	○
Told the person or people how I felt about what they were doing.	○	○	○	○
Walked away.	○	○	○	○
Told an adult at school.	○	○	○	○

Told an adult at home.	O	O	O	O
Told a friend(s).	O	O	O	O
Made a joke about it.	O	O	O	O

Other (What else did you do and how much did it help?)

33. Overall, what did you do that helped you the most?

34. What happened when you did that?

35. What else do you wish you had done?

36. What did adults at school do about what was done to you? What happened when they did those things? Please click one option for each action.

	Adults didn't do this	Adults did this and things got worse	Adults did this and there was no change	Adults did this and things got better
Gave me advice.	O	O	O	O
Listened to me.	O	O	O	O
Ignored what was going on.	O	O	O	O
Told me to solve the problem myself.	O	O	O	O
Told me to stop tattling.	O	O	O	O
Told me that if I acted differently this wouldn't happen to me.	O	O	O	O
Said they would talk with the other student or students.	O	O	O	O
Sat down with me and the other student or students together.	O	O	O	O
Used punishments for the other student(s).	O	O	O	O
Checked in with me afterwards to see if the behavior stopped.	O	O	O	O
Kept up increased adult supervision for some time.	O	O	O	O
Talked with the whole class or school about the behavior.	O	O	O	O

Brought in a speaker to talk with the whole class or school about the behavior.	○	○	○	○
Talked about the behavior in class more than once.	○	○	○	○

Other (What else did adults do and how much did it help?)

37. Overall, what did adults do that helped the most?

38. What happened when they did that?

39. What else do you wish adults had done?

40. What did other students do about what was done to you? What happened when they did that? Please click one option for each action.

	No one did this	Other students did this and things got worse	Other students did this and things didn't change	Other students did this and things got better
Told the person to stop in a mean or angry way.	○	○	○	○
Listened to me.	○	○	○	○
Asked the person to stop being mean to me in a friendly way.	○	○	○	○
Ignored what was going on.	○	○	○	○
Spent time with me, sat with me, or hung out with me.	○	○	○	○
Gave me advice about what I should do.	○	○	○	○
Blamed me for what was happening.	○	○	○	○
Made fun of me for asking for help or for being treated badly.	○	○	○	○
Called me at home to encourage me.	○	○	○	○
Talked to me at school to encourage me.	○	○	○	○
Told an adult.	○	○	○	○
Helped me tell an adult.	○	○	○	○

| Helped me get away from situations where the behavior was going on. | ○ | ○ | ○ | ○ |
| Distracted the people who were treating me badly. | ○ | ○ | ○ | ○ |

Other (What else did other students do and how much did it help?)

41. Overall, what did other students do that helped the most?

42. What happened when they did that?

43. What else do you wish other students had done?

44. What have you done to help another student be safe or have friends at school? Again, because this survey is confidential, please do NOT include any names. Thanks!

45. What happened when you did that?

Thank you so much for your help! We are very interested in what you have to say. We know that we have asked you to think about some uncomfortable behaviors. If any of the survey questions have made you feel bad in any way, please be sure to tell a teacher or another adult.

Thanks again.

References

Allday, R. A., & Pakurar, K. (2007). Effects of teacher greetings on student on-task behaviors. *Journal of Applied Behavior Analysis, 40,* 317–320.

Bandura, A. (1977). Self-efficacy: Toward a unifying theory of behavioral change. *Psychological Review, 84*(2), 191–215.

Bandura, A. (1994). Regulated function of perceived self-efficacy. In *Personnel selection and classification,* M. G. Rumsey, C. B. Walker, & J. H. Harris. (Eds.). Hillsdale, NJ: Erlbaum.

Battistich, V., Solomon, D., Watson, M., & Schaps, E. (1997). Caring school communities. *Educational Psychologist, 32*(3) 137–151.

Battistich, V., Watson, M., Solomon, D., Schaps, E., & Solomon, J. (1991a). The child development project: A comprehensive program for the development of prosocial character. In *Handbook of moral behavior and development: Vol. 1. Theory.* Hillsdale, NJ: Erlbaum.

Battistich, V., Watson, M., Solomon, D., Schaps, E., & Solomon, J. (1991b). The child development project: A comprehensive program for the development of prosocial character. In *Handbook of moral behavior and development: Vol. 2. Research.* Hillsdale, NJ: Erlbaum.

Battistich, V., Watson, M., Solomon, D., Schaps, E., & Solomon, J. (1991c). The child development project: A comprehensive program for the development of prosocial character. In *Handbook of moral behavior and development: Vol. 3: Application.* Hillsdale, NJ: Erlbaum.

Baumeister, R. F., & Leary, M. R. (1995). The need to belong: Desire for interpersonal attachments as a fundamental human motivation. *Psychological Bulletin, 117,* 497–529.

Benard, B. (1991). *Fostering resiliency in kids: Protective factors in the family, school and community.* Portland, OR: Northwest Regional Educational Laboratory.

Benson, P. L., Scales, P. C., Leffert, N., & Roehlkepartain, E. C. (1999). *A fragile foundation: The state of developmental assets among American youth.* Minneapolis: Search Institute.

Bingelli, N. (2013). *CBT techniques: Part 1. Cognitive restructuring.* Retrieved August 23, 2013, from http://www.nelsonbinggeli.net/NB/CBT-CR.html

Bjorkqvist, K., Lagerspetz, K. M., & Kaukiainen, A. (1992). Do girls manipulate and boys fight? Developmental trends in regard to direct and indirect aggression. *Aggressive Behavior, 18*, 117–127.

Blum, R. W., & Libbey, H. P. (2004). Wingspread Declaration on school connections. *Journal of School Health, 74*(7), 231–234.

Bosari, B. E., & Carey, K. B. (2000). Effects of a brief motivational intervention with college student drinkers. *Journal of Consulting and Clinical Psychology, 68*, 728–733.

Brown, B. (2004). Adolescents' relationships with peers. In R. Lerner & L. Steinberg (Eds.), *Handbook of adolescent psychology* (2nd ed.). New York: Wiley.

Card, N. A., Stucky, B. D., Sawalani, G. M., & Little, T. D. (2008). Direct and indirect aggression during childhood and adolescence: A meta-analytic review of gender differences, intercorrelations, and relations to maladjustment. *Child Development, 79*(5), 1185–1229.

Cobb, N. J. (2010). *Adolescence* (7th ed.). Sunderland, MA: Sinauer.

Commission on Children at Risk. (2003). *Hardwired to connect: The new scientific case for authoritative communities.* New York: Institute for American Values.

Committee for Children. (1997). *Second Step: A violence prevention program.* Seattle, WA: Author.

Compas, B. E., Connor-Smith, J. K., Saltzman, H., Thomsen, A. H., & Wadsworth, M. E. (2001). Coping with stress during childhood and adolescence: Problems, progress, and potential in theory and research. *Psychological Bulletin, 127*(1), 87–127.

Compas, B. E., Malcarne, V. L., & Fondacaro, K. M. (1988). Coping with stressful events in older children and young adolescents. *Journal of Consulting and Clinical Psychology, 56*, 405–411.

Crick, N. R., Grotpeter, J., & Bigbee, M. A. (2002). Relationally and physically aggressive children's intent, attributions and feelings of distress for relational and instrumental peer provocations. *Child Development, 73*(4), 1134–1142.

Crosnoe, R., Johnson, M. K., & Elder, G. H. (2004). Intergenerational bonding in school: The behavioral and contextual correlates of student-teacher relationships. *Sociology of Education, 77*(1), 60–81.

Cummings, E. M., & Davies, P. T. (1994). *Children and marital conflict: The impact of family dispute and resolution.* New York: Guilford.

Davis, S. (2007a). *Empowering bystanders in bullying prevention.* Champaign, IL: Research Press.

Davis, S. (2007b). *Schools where everyone belongs: Practical strategies for reducing bullying* (2nd ed.). Champaign, IL: Research Press.

Deci, E. L., & Flaste, R. (1996). *Why we do what we do: Understanding self-motivation.* New York: Penguin.

Deci, E. L., Koestner, R., & Ryan, M. (1999). A meta-analytic review of experiments examining the effects of rewards on intrinsic motivation. *Psychological Bulletin, 125*(6), 627–688.

Dweck, C. S. (1999). *Self-theories: Their role in motivation, personality and development.* New York: Psychology Press.

Dweck, C. S. (2006). *Mindset: The new psychology of success.* New York: Random House.

Eccles, J. S., Wigfield, A., & Schiefele, U. (1998). Motivation to succeed. In W. Damon (Series Ed.) & N. Eisenberg (Vol. Ed.), *Handbook of child psychology* (5th ed., Vol. 3). New York: Wiley.

Ekstrom, R. B., Goertz, M. E., Pollack, J. M., & Rock, D. A. (1986). Who drops out of high school and why? Findings from a national study. *Teachers College Record, 87,* 356–73.

Fagot, B. I., & Leinbach, M. D. (1989). The young child's gender schema: Environmental input, internal organization. *Child Development, 60,* 663–672.

Fried, S., & Sosland, B. (2009). *Banishing bullying behavior.* Maryland: Rowman & Littlefield.

Furman, W., & Buhrmester, D. (1992). Age and sex differences in perceptions of networks of personal relationships. *Child Development, 63,*103–115.

Gaughan, E., Cerio, J. D., & Myers, R. A. (2001). *Lethal violence in schools.* Alfred, NY: Alfred University.

Gay Lesbian Straight Education Network. (2009). *National School Climate Survey: The experiences of lesbian, gay, bisexual and transgender youth in our nation's schools.* Retrieved May 31, 2013, from http://www.glsen.org/cgi-bin/iowa/all/news/record/2897.html

Gilligan, C. (1982). New maps of development: New visions of maturity. *American Journal of Orthopsychiatry, 52*(2), 199–212.

Griffith, M. A., Dubow, E. F., & Ippolito, M. F. (2000). Developmental and cross-situational differences in adolescents' coping strategies. *Journal of Youth and Adolescence, 29*(2), 183–204.

Hatzenbuehler, M. L. (2011). The social environment and suicide attempts in lesbian, gay, and bisexual youth. *Pediatrics, 127*(5), 896–903.

Himmelstein, K. E., & Brückner, H. (2011). Criminal-justice and school sanctions against nonheterosexual youth: A longitudinal study. *Pediatrics, 127,* 49–57.

Hinduja, S., & Patchin, J. W. (2009). *Bullying beyond the schoolyard: Preventing and responding to cyberbullying.* Thousand Oaks, CA: Sage.

Holt-Lunstad, J., & Smith, T. B. (2012). Social relationships and mortality. *Social and Personality Psychology Compass, 6,* 41–53.

Hudley, C., & Graham, S. (1993). An attributional intervention to reduce peer-directed aggression among African-American boys. *Child Development, 64,* 124–138.

Janosz, M., Archambault, I., Pagani, L. S., Pascal, S., Morin, A. J. S., & Bowen, F. (2008). Are there detrimental effects of witnessing school violence in early adolescence? *Journal of Adolescent Health, 43,* 600–608.

Jaratt, C. J. (1982). *Helping children cope with separation and loss.* Boston: The Harvard Common Press.

Johnson, M. K., Crosnoe, R., & Elder, G. H. (2001). Students' attachment and academic engagement: The role of race and ethnicity. *Sociology of Education, 74*, 318–340.

Katz, J. (1999). *Tough guise: Men, violence and the crisis in masculinity* (Film). Northampton, MA: Media Education Foundation.

Klein, D. N., & Kuiper, N. A. (2006). Humor styles, peer relationships, and bullying in middle childhood. *Humor, 19*(4), 383–404.

Larson, R. W., Richards, M. H., Moneta, G., Holmbeck, G., & Duckett, E. (1996). Changes in adolescents' daily interactions with their families from ages 10 to 18: Disengagement and transformation. *Developmental Psychology, 32*, 744–754.

Levitt, M. J., Guacci-Franco, N., & Levitt, J. L. (1993). Convoys of social support in childhood and early adolescence: Structure and function. *Developmental Psychology, 29*, 811–818.

Lewis, M. A., & Neighbors, C. (2004). Gender-specific misperceptions of college student drinking norms. *Psychology of Addictive Behaviors, 18*, 334–339.

Lieber, C. M. (2002). *Partners in learning: From conflict to collaboration in secondary classrooms*. Cambridge, MA: Educators for Social Responsibility.

Litt, D. M., & Stock, M. L. (2011). Adolescent alcohol-related risk cognitions: The role of social norms and social networking sites. *Psychology of Addictive Behaviors, 25*(4), 708–713.

Martin, R. A., Puhlik-Doris, P., Larsen, G., Gray, J., & Weir, K. (2003). Individual differences in uses of humor and their relation to psychological well-being: Development of the Humor Styles Questionnaire. *Journal of Research in Personality, 37*, 48–75.

Maslow, A. H. (1943). A theory of human motivation. *Psychological Review, 50*(4), 370–396.

Maslow, A. H. (1954). *Motivation and personality*. New York: Harper.

Masten, A. S. (2001). Ordinary magic: Resilience processes in development. *American Psychologist, 56*(3), 227–238.

Masten A. S., Best K., & Garmezy, N. (1990). Resilience and development: Contributions from the study of children who overcome adversity. *Development and Psychopathology, 2*, 425–444.

Moody, J., & White, D. R. (2003). Structural cohesion and embeddedness: A hierarchical concept of social groups. *American Sociological Review, 68*(1), 103–127.

Nansel, T. R., Overpeck, M., Pilla, R. S., Ruan, W. J., Simons-Morton, B., & Scheidt, P. (2001). Bullying behaviors among U.S. youth: Prevalence and association with psychosocial adjustment. *Journal of the American Medical Association, 285*, 2094–2100.

Nixon, C. L., Linkie, C. A., Coleman, P. K., & Fitch, C. (2011). Peer relational victimization and somatic complaints during adolescence. *Journal of Adolescent Health, 49*(3), 294–299.

Olweus, D. (1993). *Bullying at school: What we know and what we can do*. Oxford, United Kingdom: Blackwell.

Olweus, D. (1997). Bully/victim problems in school: Facts and intervention. European *Journal of Psychology of Education, 12*(4), 495–510.

Orpinas, P. , & Horne, A. M. (2006). *Bullying prevention: Creating a positive school climate and developing social competence.* Washington, DC: American Psychological Association.

Patchin, J. (2012). *Peer influences and social norming.* Retrieved September, 23, 2013, from http://cyberbullying.us/peer-influences-and-social-norming/

Perkins, W. H., & Berkowitz, A. D. (1986). Perceiving the community norms of alcohol use among students: Some research implications for campus alcohol education programming. *International Journal of the Addictions, 21*(9–10), 961–976.

Peterson, C., Maier, S., & Seligman, M. E. P. (1993). *Learned helplessness: A theory for the age of personal control.* New York: Oxford University Press.

Pollack, W. S. (2004). Male adolescent rites of passage: Positive visions of multiple developmental pathways. *Annals of the New York Academy of Sciences, 1036,* 141–150.

Pollack, W. S., Modzeleski, W., & Rooney, G. (2008). *Prior knowledge of potential school-based violence: Information students learn may prevent a targeted attack* (Report from the U. S. Secret Service and U. S. Department of Education). Retrieved September 20, 2013, from http://ok.gov/sde/sites/ok.gov.sde/files/ByStanderStudy.pdf

Powlishta, K. K. (2000). The effect of target age on the activation of gender stereotypes. *Sex Roles, 42*(3–4), 271–282.

Prinstein, M. J., Boergers, J., & Vernberg, E. M. (2001). Overt and relational aggression in adolescents: Social-psychological adjustment of aggressors and victims. *Journal of Clinical Child Psychology, 30*(4), 479–491.

Resnick, M., Bearman, P., Blum, R., Bauman, K. E., Harris, K. M., Jones, J., Tabor, J., Beuhring, T., Sieving, R. E., Shew, M., Ireland, M., Bearinger, L. H., & Udry, J. R. (1997). Protecting young people from harm: Findings from the National Longitudinal Study of Adolescent Health. *Journal of the American Medical Association, 278,* 823–832.

Rivers, I. (2001). The bullying of sexual minorities at school: Its nature and long-term correlates. *Educational and Child Psychology, 18(1),* 33–46.

Ross, D. M. (2003). *Childhood bullying, teasing, and violence: What school personnel, other professionals, and parents can do.* Alexandria, VA: American Counseling Association.

Sanford, L. (2005). *Strong at the broken places: Building resiliency in survivors of trauma.* Mt. Holyoke, MA: NEARI Press.

Sapolsky, R. M. (2004). *Why zebras don't get ulcers* (3rd ed.). New York: Holt.

Scales, P. C., & Roehlkepartain, E. C. (2012). Peter Lorimer Benson (1946–2011). *American Psychologist, 67*(4), 322.

Scheithauer, H., Hayer, T., Petermann, F., & Jugert, G. (2006). Physical, verbal, and relational forms of bullying among German students: Age trends, gender differences, and correlates. *Aggressive Behavior, 32,* 261–275.

Schon, D. (1983). *The reflective practitioner: How professionals think in action.* New York: Basic Books.

Selman, R. L. (1980). *The growth of interpersonal understanding: Clinical and developmental analyses.* New York: Academic.

Shure, M. B. (2000). *I Can Problem Solve: An interpersonal cognitive problem-solving program—Kindergarten and primary grades.* Champaign, IL: Research Press.

Shure, M. B. (2001a). *I Can Problem Solve: An interpersonal cognitive problem-solving program—Intermediate elementary grades.* Champaign, IL: Research Press.

Shure, M. B. (2001b). *I Can Problem Solve: An interpersonal cognitive problem-solving program—Preschool.* Champaign, IL: Research Press.

Shure, M. B., & Spivack, G. (1980). Interpersonal problem solving as a mediator of behavioral adjustment in preschool and kindergarten children. *Journal of Applied Developmental Psychology, 1,* 29–44.

Shure, M. B., & Spivack, G. (1982). Interpersonal problem-solving in young children: A cognitive approach to prevention. *American Journal of Community Psychology, 10,* 341–356.

Skiba, R. J., Michael, R. S., Nardo, A. C., & Peterson, R. L. (2002). The color of discipline: Sources of racial and gender disproportionality in school punishment. *Urban Review, 34,* 317–342.

Solberg, M. E., & Olweus, D. (2003). Prevalence estimation of school bullying with the Olweus Bully/Victim Questionnaire. *Aggressive Behavior, 29,* 239–268.

Steinberg, L., & Silverberg, S. (1986). The vicissitudes of autonomy in early adolescence. *Child Development, 57,* 841–851.

Smith, P. K., Morita, Y., Junger-Tas, J., Olweus, D., Catalano, R., & Slee, P. (Eds.). (1999). *The nature of school bullying: A cross-national perspective.* New York: Routledge.

Visser, C. (2006). *Interview with Carol Dweck.* Retrieved September 20, 2013, from http://interviewscoertvisser.blogspot.com/2007/11/interview with-carol-dweck_4897.html

Weinstein, L., Laverghetta, A., Alexander, R., & Stewart, M. (2009). Teacher greetings increase college students' test scores. *College Student Journal, 43*(2), 452–453.

Werner, E., & Smith, R. (1989). *Vulnerable but invincible: A longitudinal study of resilient children and youth.* New York: Adams, Bannister, and Cox.

Whitlock, J. L. (2006). Youth perceptions of life at school: Contextual correlates of school connectedness in adolescence. *Applied Developmental Science, 10*(1), 13–29.

Williams, K. D. (1997). Social ostracism. In R. M. Kowalski (Ed.), *Aversive interpersonal behaviors.* New York: Plenum.

Williams, K. D. (2001). *Ostracism: The power of silence.* New York: Guilford.

Wilson, M. B. (2011). *What to do about tattling.* Retrieved September 20, 2013, from https://www.responsiveclassroom.org/article/what-to-do-about-tattling

Yeager, D. S, Miu, A. S., Powers, J., & Dweck, C. S. (2013). Implicit theories of personality and attributions of hostile intent: A meta-analysis, an experiment, and a longitudinal intervention. *Child Development, 84*(5), 1651.

Yeager, D. S., Trzesniewski, K. H., Tirri, K., Nokelainen, P., & Dweck, C. S. (2011). Adolescents' implicit theories predict desire for vengeance after peer conflicts: Correlational and experimental evidence. *Developmental Psychology, 47*(4), 1090–1107.

Young, A. L. (2011). *Queer youth advice for educators: How to respect and protect your lesbian, gay, bisexual and transgender students.* Providence, RI: Next Generation Press.

Yurgelun-Todd, D. (2007). Emotional and cognitive changes during adolescence. *Current Opinion in Neurobiology,17*(2), 251–257.

About the Authors

Stan Davis worked as a social worker and child and family therapist for 20 years and then became a school guidance counselor. In that capacity, he worked at grade levels K-12 for another 23 years until he retired from counseling in 2011. He became focused on bullying prevention in the late 1980s while working in schools and developed a range of school-based techniques focused on the research of Dan Olweus, Dorothea Ross, Myrna Shure, Carol Dweck, and others. He began training educators and consulting with schools in the late 1990s and has continued to the present, working with schools all over the United States, in Canada, throughout West Africa, and in India. He is the author of two previous books, *Schools Where Everyone Belongs* and *Empowering Bystanders in Bullying Prevention* (both published by Research Press). Stan was a founding board member of the International Bullying Prevention Association and maintains the website stopbullyingnow.com

Charisse L. Nixon received her PhD in developmental psychology from West Virginia University and is currently an associate professor of psychology at Penn State Erie. Her primary research interest focuses on all forms of peer mistreatment, including both relational and physical mistreatment. Charisse is currently studying effective prevention and intervention efforts designed to reduce peer mistreatment and its associated harm. Building students' resiliency is a core tenet of her work. She continues to train educators and students throughout the United States and Canada. Charisse's work has been featured in many national venues, as well as published in several peer-reviewed journals. She is coauthor of the book *Girls Wars: 12 Strategies That Will End Female Bullying.*